We believe Dallas would have been deeply honored to see his voice included in this instructive blending of spiritual wisdom that seamlessly spans centuries, continents, and cultures. In *Seeking God*, the wisdom of Hudson, Willard, and Ignatius flows together in ways that resonate and harmonize to provide us with time-tested, grace-fueled practical steps we can take as we seek

JANE WILLARD and REBECCA WILLARI
Dallas Willard Ministries

Trevor Hudson is a dear friend, and his friendship has been a great gift. *Seeking God* is about how to seek and find a life of intimate friendship with the creator of the universe. This important book is a culmination of Trevor having lived the insights he's gained from two of his dear friends, Dallas Willard and Ignatius of Loyola. Trust your deepest desires—and the wisdom of this author—and you'll find that you are living another kind of life.

GARY W. MOON, MDIV, PHD, founding executive director of the Martin Institute for Christianity and Culture and the Dallas Willard Center at Westmont College and author of *Apprenticeship with Jesus* and *Becoming Dallas Willard*

This is the book I needed to read in this season. The wisdom of Ignatius has been part of my life for more than two decades, and I have explored Dallas Willard's writing for about half that time. There is very little new to me conceptually in this book. And yet—Trevor Hudson's extraordinary distillation and simple explanation has moved me. Hudson has a remarkable gift, true to his Methodist roots, of making things accessible to the person in the pew. I found my heart stirred and myself challenged in ways that took me to conversation with Jesus. I would heartily recommend this book to anyone who has chosen to commit their life to companionship with Jesus.

MAGS BLACKIE, PHD, spiritual director and author of *Rooted in Love* and *The Grace of Forgiveness*

This book cannot be read well all at once. Every page brings with it an invitation to encounter the risen Lord—the source of abundant, eternal life, which begins in the here and now. Drawing on the Exercises of Ignatius and the wisdom of Dallas Willard, Trevor Hudson invites us to experience for ourselves the power of the present Christ, who calls us by name and transforms our lives.

PAUL N. ANDERSON, professor of biblical and Quaker studies at George Fox University

I thank God for *Seeking God*. In it Trevor Hudson invites us into a life-altering journey of seeking and enlists the help of two profound individuals, Ignatius of Loyola and Dallas Willard. Both have learned to live deeply "in the house of [their] own teaching," and they are genuine companions in the Way even though they lived centuries apart. Read *Seeking God*. Practice *Seeking God*. Live *Seeking God*.

RICHARD J. FOSTER, author of several books, including *Celebration of Discipline* and *Sanctuary of the Soul*

In *Seeking God*, pastor and spiritual teacher Trevor Hudson writes with grace-filled honesty and vulnerability, pastoring readers toward a deeper spiritual life while anchoring us in our profound belovedness along the way. The spiritual exercises described in each chapter gently invite readers to remove any barriers of obligation, guilt, or performance and instead reimagine, receive, and enjoy intimacy with God in tangible and creative ways. Trevor's compassionate voice, spiritual insights, and pastoral wisdom are a gift for all of us who are longing for a more vibrant life with God.

CHRISTINE YI SUH, pastor, spiritual director, and author of *Forty Days on Being a Four*

Jesus promises us an abundant life through him (John 10:10), and Trever Hudson's *Seeking God* is a thoughtful and heartfelt guide to the way of Christ. This alone is reason to read this book, but the fact that Hudson also skillfully weaves into his writing the wisdom of two great spiritual teachers—Ignatius of Loyola and Dallas Willard—makes this book even more of a gift.

CARL MCCOLMAN, author of *Eternal Heart* and *Unteachable Lessons*

I found myself riveted by this book, in which Trevor Hudson invites us to seek and find another kind of life, the resurrection life of deep fulfillment and joy that God desires us to experience here and now. He helps us with the how by drawing on formative encounters in his own life with two God seekers, sixteenth-century Saint Ignatius of Loyola (through his *Spiritual Exercises*) and philosopher and spiritual writer of our own time Dallas Willard. Through Trevor's words the wisdom of these two seekers comes alive in a remarkable and deeply personal way that transforms how we see the ordinary and the everyday. It is a particular gift to be given access to some of the personal conversations and letters between Hudson and Willard and to see how the perspectives and wisdom of Ignatius and Willard interpenetrate and offer us a vision of hope and possibility for living differently. This is a book to be prayerfully read, savored, and reread often.

ANNEMARIE PAULIN-CAMPBELL, PHD, head of the Jesuit Institute School of Spirituality in South Africa and coauthor of the revision of *The Spiritual Exercises Reclaimed*

I don't know anyone with more spiritual wisdom than Trevor Hudson. Trevor's godliness is on full display in *Seeking God: Finding Another Kind of Life with St. Ignatius and Dallas Willard*. Seeking is not just the way into faith; it is the way on. Only a passionate seeker of God like Trevor can pass on the gems in this book from Ignatius and Willard. Trevor generates spiritual thirst in seekers and leads them to Living Water.

DR. TODD HUNTER, Anglican bishop and author of *Deep Peace*

Trevor Hudson knows that each one of us is on a seeking journey. Whether we've been Christ followers for decades or are newly intrigued by Jesus of Nazareth, we are all looking for the good news that promises another kind of life. In this wonderfully invitational book, Trevor leads us through the contours of the Ignatian Exercises, introducing us to Ignatius himself and to Dallas Willard as wise companions in our seeking. Trevor's honest life experiences with Jesus kindle a lasting hope for all of us longing for a deeper life with God. Trevor's compassionate and compelling tone sets a table and invites us to "come and see." If you are longing for a deeper life with God, if you have a wondering hunger to meet Jesus, this book is for you.

LACY BORGO, spiritual director and teacher

Skillfully drawing wisdom from a sixteenth-century Catholic saint, Ignatius of Loyola; a twenty-first-century philosopher and Christian spiritual writer, Dallas Willard; and the narrative of his own life, Trevor Hudson accompanies others in their search for God. Every page of this book offers wisdom drawn from the lives of these three spiritual guides. Every age needs holy men and women to seek Jesus and be a witness for him. Ignatius and Dallas responded to this call for their contemporaries, and with them as his companions, Trevor does the same for us today. Trevor is a man of God's church, following Christ humbly and faithfully. Transcending the boundaries of denomination, he is a true ecumenist, offering anybody who is seeking a sure way of finding God. Trevor makes this wisdom accessible because he shares so much of his own heart, life, faith, experience, and discipleship. I could not put this book down—one of my favorites of Trevor's!

FATHER RUSSELL POLLITT, SJ, director of the Jesuit Institute South Africa

If I had to choose one person to turn to for wisdom on seeking God in a deep, helpful, discerning way, it would be Trevor Hudson. Trevor's new book, *Seeking God*, contains the wisdom and writing of a modern master of spiritual formation. If you read one book this year on nurturing your life with God, let *Seeking God* be the one. Very highly recommended!

CHRIS HALL, PHD, former president of Renovaré and distinguished professor emeritus of theology at Eastern University

Seeking
-God-

FINDING ANOTHER KIND OF LIFE

WITH ST. IGNATIUS

AND DALLAS WILLARD

TREVOR HUDSON

A NavPress resource published in alliance
with Tyndale House Publishers

NavPress ⬤

NavPress is the publishing ministry of The Navigators, an international Christian organization and leader in personal spiritual development. NavPress is committed to helping people grow spiritually and enjoy lives of meaning and hope through personal and group resources that are biblically rooted, culturally relevant, and highly practical.

For more information, visit NavPress.com.

The Team:
David Zimmerman, Publisher; Deborah Sáenz Gonzalez, Acquisitions Editor; Elizabeth Schroll, Copy Editor; Olivia Eldredge, Operations Manager; Ron Kaufmann, Designer

To Debbie—my closest companion along the Way, who first suggested that I write about the seeking life.

CONTENTS

FOREWORD

IN *SEEKING GOD*, Trevor Hudson offers readers the fruit of years of praying, reading, teaching, and ministering to readers who are experiencing the desire for something more in their lives. That desire for "something more" has been planted deep in their hearts by their Creator. God has, from the arrival of human beings, wanted our friendship, and as a result of that desire, deep in the heart of every human being is a reciprocal desire for friendship with God. As you will find out in this book, Trevor Hudson himself has been taken with that desire for friendship with God all his adult life. Friendship with God has brought him great joy and deep happiness.

He calls the kind of life that includes a deep friendship with God "*zoe* life." *Zoe* is the Greek word for life in the New Testament. Hudson uses this word to distinguish what God offers us from other ways of life that do not include friendship with God.

So, if you experience a desire for a deeper kind of life than you presently have, you have picked up a book that will help you. As I noted, Hudson himself has been seeking God all his adult life. In that seeking, he found the most help from two sources: his friendship with a great teacher and philosopher, the late Dallas Willard; and Ignatius of Loyola, the sixteenth-century Spanish founder of the Society of Jesus (the Jesuits) and, more importantly for Trevor Hudson, the author of the *Spiritual Exercises*. If you take the invitation Hudson offers, you will spend a great deal of time with the spiritualities of these two sources, and both will help you to grow into the friendship with God that God himself wants.

I first met Trevor Hudson because of his seeking nature. He had come upon some of my writing and, on a trip to the United States, asked if I would lead him on an eight-day retreat. I gladly agreed to take him on. Since that time, we have been in touch by email. I consider him a friend in Christ. As he was writing this book, he asked me to review the chapters as he wrote them. I gladly agreed and have found the book insightful and inviting. Hence, I am happy to write this foreword and recommend the book to you.

Before reading this manuscript, I knew little about Dallas Willard. Trevor Hudson brings him to life here. You will meet a very holy but down-to-earth man in these pages. And I believe you will find yourself attracted to the kind of friendship with God that Willard himself seems to have enjoyed.

As a Jesuit for seventy years this August, I already knew a good deal about Ignatius's *Spiritual Exercises*, a book of instructions for someone who will lead others into a deeper relationship with God. Trevor Hudson not only did the *Spiritual Exercises* but has also mastered the inner dynamic that powers them and that has proven helpful to people for half a millennium. Hudson uses the structure of the Exercises to help readers develop a deep, personal relationship with God that will not only change their prayer life but will also move them to a deeper commitment to cooperating with God in the great project begun with the creation of this universe.

You are in good hands on this journey with Trevor Hudson. Let's give God the joy of deepening our friendship with him. As we do, we'll increase our own happiness and participate in building up what Jesus called "the Kingdom of God."

William Barry, SJ

CHAPTER 1

BECOMING A SEEKER

I encourage you to seek the Lord constantly,
and the experiences will come along.

DALLAS WILLARD
Personal Correspondence

THIS BOOK IS ABOUT SEEKING and finding another kind of life.

As a pastor, I often sense this quest hidden in my conversations with others. People will seldom explicitly say, "I am looking for another kind of life." I do, however, hear phrases like these:

- "There's something missing in my life."
- "My life is such a mess."
- "Is this really what it's all about?"
- "Surely, there must be more to my faith than what I am experiencing."

- "I'm not getting much out of going to church right now."
- "I've given up on organized religion."

Each time sentiments like these are expressed, I hear echoes of the longing to find another kind of life. And it's a longing I well understand.

Some time ago, Debbie, my dear marriage partner of over forty years, said to me, "Ever since I've known you, you've been a spiritual seeker." She was right. For over forty years, my life has been shaped around my search for the life that I have glimpsed in the stories of those early followers of Jesus on the pages of the New Testament.

Since you have picked up this book, I assume you are willing to join me in seeking another kind of life. Each of us must make our own way through the maze of questions, the mystery, and the paradoxes that life brings us, but the gospel promises us that those who seek will find (Matthew 7:7). Only those open to becoming intentional seekers discover the radiant life that God wants to give us.

My prayer is that as you read this book, God will surprise you in your seeking and draw you more deeply into the fullness of life that is the promise of the gospel.

Encouragement for the Seeking Journey

As we begin this seeking journey together, we receive much encouragement from the Scriptures. Here are three verses to get us started:

When you search for me, you will find me; if you
seek me with all your heart, I will let you find me,
says the LORD.

JEREMIAH 29:13-14

Seek first his kingdom and his righteousness, and
all these things will be given to you as well.

MATTHEW 6:33, NIV

Ask and it will be given to you; seek and you will
find; knock and the door will be opened to you. For
everyone who asks receives; the one who seeks finds;
and to the one who knocks, the door will be opened.

MATTHEW 7:7-8, NIV

The promise is clear. Those who seek God consistently,
faithfully, and passionately will not be disappointed. They
will find God and all those good things that accompany
God's Kingdom.

We really need to grasp this because we have a tragic tendency to regard only those who are outside the Christian faith
as seekers. We then assume that once someone gives their life
to Christ, their seeking comes to an end. It is exactly the
opposite. That is when the quest really begins. Christianity
is essentially a seeking faith.

So an important question at the outset of our journey is
this: *Are you willing to take these biblical invitations to seek God
seriously?* I hope you will.

When it comes to spiritual seeking, we can learn a lot from dedicated scientists. They often spend a lifetime searching to unlock the mysterious secrets of the physical world around us. Most of the greatest discoveries have been made by scientists who refused to give up seeking. Often these breakthroughs of scientific knowledge are made by those who do not lose a childlike sense of wonder and exploration. For example, even though Einstein struggled with dyslexia, he nurtured a delightfully childlike quality of seeking throughout his life.

Surely, given the even greater mystery of God, and the unseen realities of God's Kingdom, we need to follow their example. When we cease seeking, we find ourselves in danger of dying spiritually. Our faith gets bogged down in dull familiarity, empty routines, and tired clichés. In stark contrast, becoming a seeker brings us alive spiritually. We come alive to the mystery of ourselves, of those around us, of the world in which we live, and above all, of the active presence of God permeating all things. Few invitations are more important than the biblical one to seek God and the life that God wants to give us. This is the essence of the spiritual quest that we will explore in this book.

Even more than scientists, the great Christ followers throughout history encourage us to keep on seeking. From Paul in the New Testament onward, we meet wonderful people of faith who gave themselves to a lifetime of searching. When we study their lives, no matter whether they were Protestant or Catholic or Orthodox, the one thing that becomes clear is that they continually sought God. These men and women remind us that when we seek God resolutely, we will find God to be real and active in our lives. Indeed, God will come to us and communicate the divine Trinitarian reality in all its glory, beauty, and power. We will discover another kind of life.

Keeping Jesus at the Center

My own seeking journey with God has continued now for just over fifty years. As with all intimate and growing friendships, there have been many highs and lows. Almost daily I am confronted with the inadequacies of my own life with God. I still find myself struggling with discouraging symptoms of self-centeredness, self-interest, and egocentricity. There has, however, been one unrelenting constant that has both encouraged and guided my own seeking: the shining figure of Jesus of Nazareth.

My spiritual seeking began in my teenage years. As a sixteen-year-old, I was very aware of the preciousness of this one life. I wanted it to count for something. Thankfully, I met Phillip, a young Christ follower who sat next to me at school. There was something different about his life—not weirdly different but rather attractively different.

When I asked him about this difference, he introduced me to his friendship with Jesus Christ. He shared with me how Jesus gave his life on the cross for us, told me about how he lives now beyond crucifixion, and explained how the Spirit can give us new life today. Phillip went on to say that if

I wanted to experience this new life, I needed to turn toward Christ and give my life to him.

This basic, street-level gospel shone a bright light into my heart. Late one night, as I was walking down Havelock Street in my hometown of Port Elizabeth, Eastern Cape, South Africa, I made my decision. I recall looking up at the sky and saying something like "Lord Jesus Christ, thank you for everything you have done for me because of your love. Please come into my life and make me the person you want me to be." That teenage moment of inner surrender to the crucified love of God shaped the rest of my life.

My journey with Jesus, and into the fullness of life God gives, had begun. For the past fifty years, that Christ light has continued to be my encouraging and guiding presence as I have sought to follow Jesus into the life of the Kingdom of God, here and now.

Now you can see why, as we reach out for the life that God gives us, I want us to stay close to Jesus. On any seeking journey it is easy to lose our way. Thankfully, Jesus lights the path for our steps along the way. Through his words and deeds, his death and resurrection, he offers himself as the one who uniquely leads us into the life of his Father's Kingdom.

This is the astonishing mystery of our life with God: The way into it is simply through coming to know, love, and follow Jesus Christ. As we learn to keep company with him daily, he steps out from the pages of the Gospels and becomes for us a living and empowering presence. Step by step, he

leads us into the fullness of life that is the astounding promise
of the gospel.

Learning from Two God Seekers

On our seeking journey together, we will explore the wisdom
of two God seekers who powerfully influenced their respec-
tive generations, many centuries apart.

Ignatius of Loyola (1491–1556)

In 1990 I experienced a major vocational disappointment. As
a result, I needed to make critical decisions about my future.
Not wanting to rush into premature decisions, I was encouraged by an Anglican sister to do the *Spiritual Exercises* of
Saint Ignatius. Let me be honest and say I had no idea what
they involved! Sister Maureen suggested that I ask Father
Andrew Norton, an Anglican monk from the Community of
the Resurrection, to explain them to me. I will never forget
his surprise when I knocked on his door and asked him to
take me through the Exercises.

At the end of my first visit, he said to me, "I don't
know what a high-church Anglican like me is doing with a
low-church Methodist like you. God must have a sense of
humor."

So began my adventure with Ignatius. It has been almost
thirty years since that pilgrimage through the *Spiritual
Exercises*. Since then, I have learned a great deal more about
them and about Ignatius, who first put them together. Not
only have I had the privilege of giving the Exercises to many

others, but it has also been a special joy, in recent years with the local Jesuit family here in Johannesburg, to train others to give them.

What has struck me is how, when they are suitably adapted, they connect with Christ followers from across denominational tribes. Whether you are Catholic or Protestant, mainline or independent, charismatic or Reformed, or have no formal church background at all, they seem to strike a responsive chord in the hearts of anyone eager to seek God more radically and wholeheartedly.

I hope that you will enjoy getting to know Ignatius. Although he did a few things that look a bit crazy from our twenty-first-century perspective, he also had a huge heart for God that captures our seeking imagination. He longed for those around him to give themselves freely and generously to following Jesus. The *Spiritual Exercises* that he put together reveal a profound spiritual and psychological wisdom that is remarkably adaptable. It comes as little surprise that so many contemporary seekers find him to be a reliable and helpful guide for the journey into the life God graciously offers.

Dallas Willard (1935–2013)

My first introduction to Dallas was in 1985. I was in bed, sick with mumps, when I listened to an audio cassette of his teaching on the Kingdom of God. Something in his teaching struck a deep, responsive chord in me. As I listened to him explore the themes of the availability of the Kingdom of God, the realness of the spiritual dimension, and the connections between discipleship, daily life, and mission, the flame of my longing to know, love, and follow Jesus burned brighter.

I knew that I had so much more to learn from Dallas. So I wrote a letter, inviting him to come to South Africa and spend some time teaching in the congregation where I pastored. I said I could raise his airfare but could not offer hotel accommodation or promise an honorarium. It certainly was not an attractive offer.

To my surprise and delight, Dallas responded positively to this request from a stranger. Nor, he said, did we have to worry about payment.

What struck me most, during his three weeks with us, was not so much his words. It was his life. He lived in the house of his own teaching. Like many others, I was struck by his unhurried, attentive, and compassionate presence. One reason I took his insightful ideas about God and God's Kingdom with absolute seriousness was that he obviously lived in these invisible realities himself. He was a credible witness.

Over the next twenty-five years, it was my privilege to learn from Dallas in many ways. He ministered in South Africa three more times, wrote helpful books on the life of faith, and continued lecturing in his home country. I read whatever I could get my hands on, listened to his recorded talks, and went over and over my notes from his time with us. It was, however, through personal conversation and correspondence that I learned the most from him.

In one letter, dated May 2, 1995, he responded to my longing for a deeper experience of a living, present, and personal God with this counsel:

> *I encourage you to seek the face of the Lord constantly,*
> *with the knowledge that experiences will come along. You*
> *should experience God. I would be nothing and have no*
> *faith apart from various experiences of God that have*
> *come to me. You should expect experiences and make*
> *yourself available to them. To seek them is just misguided,*
> *not wrong. We have no idea of what ours will be like,*
> *and they certainly will be unlike anyone else's.*

Throughout this book, I will share some of the faith lessons I learned from both Ignatius and Dallas. It will become clear that, although they speak to us from different centuries, Ignatius and Dallas had much in common. Both were convinced that invisible things like the Trinity, the Kingdom of God, and the soul are as real as the coffee and toast that we have for breakfast.

Both stressed that, through direct interaction, God can be experienced as a knowable, personal, and loving reality. Both believed that we can be transformed into the compassionate character of Jesus. Above all, both were adamant that the greatest opportunity in life is to come to know Jesus intimately, love him more deeply, and follow him more closely. For these reasons, and several more, both Ignatius and Dallas make ideal companions for our seeking journey.

The *Spiritual Exercises* of Saint Ignatius

The structure of this book has been significantly shaped by the major themes of the *Spiritual Exercises*. The Exercises follow a careful plan that is based on Ignatius's own experience of spiritual seeking. These central themes revolve around the relationship between God's good news and our own deepest desires, the astounding reality of God's personal love reaching out to each one of us in our sinfulness, the life and ministry of Jesus, his death and resurrection, and the active presence of God permeating and filling all things.

These themes offer themselves as signposts that can guide us in our spiritual search. Seekers always need some practical guidance, and I hope that you will find the insights from the Exercises as helpful in your spiritual seeking as I have in mine.

The *Spiritual Exercises* also connect with seekers outside the institutional church.

Recently I came across the moving testimony of the gifted actor Andrew Garfield.[1] As he prepared for his role as a Jesuit priest in Martin Scorsese's haunting film *Silence*, he asked popular Catholic author Father James Martin to take him through the *Spiritual Exercises*. Although Father Martin was initially reluctant, he sensed that Garfield was really seeking for something more in his life. His intuition was spot-on. For almost a year, Father Martin took the actor through this journey of gospel-based, Christ-centered meditations that millions of other seekers have done.

In an interview with *America Magazine*, Garfield shared the life-changing effects of this prayer journey: "There were so many things in the Exercises that changed me and transformed me, that showed me who I was . . . and where I believe God wants me to be. . . . What was really easy was falling in love with this person, was falling in love with Jesus Christ. That was the most surprising thing."

The interviewer described how, as he said these words, Garfield became quiet, obviously deeply moved. Then, pressing his hand on his chest between his stomach and his heart, he joyfully exclaimed: "That was the most remarkable thing—falling in love, and how easy it was to fall in love with Jesus. . . . I felt so bad for [Jesus] and angry on his behalf when I finally did meet him, because everyone has given him such a bad name. . . . And he has been used for so many dark things."

Like all seekers, like you and me, Garfield was seeking to discover his own unique place and purpose in this world. He went on in the interview to share himself vulnerably: "The main thing that I wanted to heal, that I brought to Jesus, that I brought to the Exercises, was this feeling of not-enough-ness. This feeling of that forever longing for the perfect expression of this thing that is inside each of us. . . . That wound of feeling like what I have to offer is never enough."

I find Garfield's testimony profoundly moving. It is a poignant testimony to how God, through the *Spiritual Exercises*, can lead a seeker in their unique faith journey from shallowness to depth.

This could also be why Dallas Willard once suggested that they make an excellent template for a school of discipleship. He wrote, "If you . . . make necessary adjustments to the content . . . you will see that [the *Spiritual Exercises*] offer in substance . . . a curriculum, a course in training, for life on the rock. And that is why, century after century, they have exercised incredible power over all who open themselves to them as disciples of Jesus."[2]

Two Important Disclaimers

In using the *Spiritual Exercises* of Saint Ignatius as an outline for our seeking journey, I must make two important disclaimers:

First, in this book I will not be taking you through the *Spiritual Exercises*. Your appetite, though, may be whetted to explore the possibilities of doing them. They are best given in a one-on-one relationship by someone trained to give them, either in a thirty-day, enclosed retreat setting or in daily life (as I did them) over a period of about nine months. What I do here is only weaving a few of their dominant themes, together with my own reflections, into the shape of this book. Hopefully, they will guide our steps along the way into a more interactive life in God's Kingdom.

Second, I am not encouraging you to read the *Spiritual Exercises*. Some of the classic works on Christian spirituality from the past, books like Brother Lawrence's *The Practice of the Presence of God*, or Mother Julian's *Revelations of Divine Love*, or John Wesley's *Forty-Four Sermons*, are meant to be slowly read, digested, and meditated on. The book on the *Spiritual Exercises*, however, is different. Like any book of exercises, it is not meant to be read but rather to be done. In fact, if you do decide to read them, you will most probably find that it is like reading a boring instruction manual. Remember always that the *Spiritual Exercises* are meant to be done, not read.

Finally, if you have read any of my previous books, you will know how I constantly emphasize the importance of action. Throughout this book you will find some suggested "Seeking Exercises." These are designed to facilitate your own personal interaction with God around some of the themes in the *Spiritual Exercises*. They are simple and will not take much time, but they will require intention, desire, and effort. Engage them with whatever trust and faith in God you have, and the God who seeks you, far more than you seek him, will surely meet you and lead you along the way into another kind of life.

As we begin our seeking journey together, here is a prayer for you. It was the first prayer that Dallas prayed when he met with a small group of seekers in South Africa. Later I learned that he would often pray these words with those he taught:

*I pray that you would have a rich life
of joy and power, abundant in
supernatural results, with a constant,
clear vision of never-ending life in
God's world before you, and of the
everlasting significance of your work,
day by day. A radiant life and death.*

CHAPTER 2

SEEKING THE LIFE GOD GIVES

The obviously well-kept secret of the "ordinary" is that it is made to be a receptacle of the divine, a place where the life of God flows.

DALLAS WILLARD

DO YOU EVER WONDER whether there is more to the life that you experience right now? Could there be a greater depth, a deeper purpose, a fuller joy to what you know presently? Is what you are experiencing in your life of faith all there is? Are you perhaps missing what your life was intended to mean?

Wonderings like these follow us around and will not let us go, even when we try to ignore them. This sense of nagging incompletion keeps us seeking for something more that will make our life fulfilling and purposeful. There seems to be at the center of our being an insatiable yearning, a relentless longing, a restless desire for a newness of life that we often struggle to clearly describe.

John H. was a recovering alcoholic who strongly believed that there is something more. Almost every month, for over fifteen years, we had lunch together. Once he told me about the first time he visited a couple struggling with addiction.

A young girl dressed in a tattered and torn dress opened the door. She led him into an untidy kitchen, the smell of stale booze in the air, where her parents were seated around the kitchen table. Obviously dealing with the effects of a terrible hangover, they invited him to sit down. John didn't know what to say. He silently asked God for help.

Then a simple sentence formed in his mind. He said to them, "It doesn't have to be this way."

I have never forgotten those words. They are wonderfully inviting, hopeful, and life-giving.

For a moment, think about the idea these words convey. They communicate possibility and potential. We do not have to be stuck forever in destructive patterns of living. We do not need to be defined permanently by past failures and mistakes. Our struggling relationships can breathe with life again. We can find freedom from the bondage of addiction. The worst thing that has happened does not have to be the last thing. Just because things get broken, they don't have to stay that way. Something beautiful, something good, can be born. Life can become wonderfully different.

It doesn't have to be this way.

There have been many times in my life when I have needed to hear those same words. I recall when I struggled with the destructive consequences of a gambling addiction

in my twenties; when Debbie and I have battled with cold-
ness and distance in our marriage; when I have felt a terrible
weariness and fatigue that comes from compulsive busyness;
when I succumbed to living with a habit of negativity rather
than a habit of happiness; when I have gotten sucked into
the pressures of performance and pleasing in my ministry;
when my relationship with God has felt barren and distant;
and the list goes on and on. These were desperate, despairing,
and dark times when I needed to know that there is another
way to live.

It doesn't have to be this way.

As I get older, those words still speak powerfully to me.
Our youth-oriented society does not encourage a hopeful
outlook on getting old. Our surrounding culture often communicates the message that when you are in your seventh
decade, you don't have much significant contribution left.
The best one can hope for is a nice retirement home, or
more golf, or more travel. So it has become crucial for me to
develop an alternative view around this critical stage of my
life's journey, one that is more inviting and hopeful. In all
the diminishments, crises, and opportunities that come with
aging, I need to hold my friend's words closely in my heart.

It doesn't have to be this way.

My country, South Africa, needs to hear these words.
When we became a democracy in 1994, our collective national
hopes for a brighter and better future for all South Africans
soared. Today, those dreams have been smashed by increasing
inequalities between the haves and the have-nots, the violent

crime that keeps us imprisoned behind electric fences, the corruption of political leaders and corporate executives in amassing great wealth at the expense of the poor, gender-based violence that has scarred the lives of countless women, and a painful racism and tribalism that seems entrenched in the ways we relate to each other. Amid this paralyzing disillusionment and disappointment, our nation desperately needs to know that the future can be different. And not only South Africa but also other nations with their own tragic pasts.

It doesn't have to be this way.

Our personal and political lives intersect in our day-to-day life with God. As I am sure you know, for all of us there come times when our faith loses its sense of edgy adventure and gets stuck in a deadening familiarity. Think of how easy it is to go through all the usual motions of worshiping God without knowing the reality of God; to accumulate insights about God without encountering God; to express beliefs in God without surrendering to God; to talk about God without following God. Again, my friend's words speak to our condition.

It doesn't have to be this way.

Right now, I wonder how my friend's words connect with where you are.

SEEKING EXERCISE

Take a moment to think about what's going on in your life right now—in your relationships with loved ones, in your work

and calling, in the challenges of your community, and
in your friendship with God. Honestly facing the current
facts of our lives makes possible new beginnings in our
relationships with God and each other. What one word would
describe the general mood of your life and faith right now?
Tell God why you choose this word, and ask God to shed light
on what your next step along the seeking path may look like.

———————————

God always draws the starting line for our fresh start right where we are. Wherever we may be standing in life right now is exactly where God's grace and mercy meet us. Even more wonderfully, we discover that when God reaches out to us in Jesus Christ, God does so with the offer of astonishing good news.

God's Good News
How would you headline the good news that Jesus announced?

Recently, I asked several people that question. Here are the top five responses I received:

- "Our sins have been forgiven."
- "We can have peace with God."
- "We are accepted as we are."
- "We are loved by God."
- "We will go to heaven when we die."

Now, each of these headlines certainly rates as good news. There is much truth in them all. But they are simply not true enough. The good news announced by Jesus is much bigger, much fuller, and much, much better.

Let us go back to that dramatic, curtain-opening moment in Jesus' ministry when he entered Galilee. Almost thirty years of hidden preparation lay behind him. Then, as he emerged from his encounter with the evil one in the wilderness, Jesus started out on his life's work. Mark the Gospel writer headlined the good news in Jesus' first public sermon in this way: "Jesus came to Galilee, proclaiming the good news of God, and saying, 'The time is fulfilled, and the kingdom of God has come near; repent, and believe in the good news'" (Mark 1:14-15).

For over forty years as a preacher, I have wrestled with how to communicate this explosive good news in street language. For most people with whom I mix, the phrase *the Kingdom of God* just doesn't connect meaningfully. It often suggests in people's minds the idea of a place far away where God rules, or a place where we go in the future where God is in charge. Seldom has this phrase sounded like really, really good news. What people miss, I think, is a felt connection between this biblical phrase and the realities of their life today.

So, how would I headline the good news to better connect with those around me?

Here is the best that I can do for the moment: *Another kind of life is available.* This is the stunning offer that lies at the heart of Jesus' message about the Kingdom of God coming near. Jesus brings not so much a new piece of advice, or a new kind of spirituality, or a new social agenda, but *a new kind of life*.

My friend was right. Life doesn't need to be this way at all. Another kind of life *is* available. Right where we are. Not only for you and me but for the whole world!

The main reason I choose the word *life* is because of the frequent way it gets used throughout the New Testament to describe the good news. In John's Gospel, we read Jesus' words: "I came that they may have life, and have it abundantly" (John 10:10). In his first epistle John writes, "God gave us eternal life, and this life is in his Son" (1 John 5:11). The next line states that "whoever has the Son has life" (verse 12).

This life that Jesus came to bring us through his life, death, and resurrection is God's very own life. It is not life that we enter only after we die; it is life that God wants to give us *in the present*. Nor do we have to travel to some special, faraway place to receive it. We can receive it *where we are*, in our ordinary, everyday lives. This eternal life, the life of the Kingdom of God, is what the risen Jesus makes available to you and me right now, right here.

The Bible speaks of two kinds of life. First, there is *bios* life. This means biological life, referring to the human, mortal, and impermanent life which all of us have been given. Second, there is *zoe* life. This means spiritual life, referring to the divine, unceasing, and indestructible life that God alone can impart to us.

This second, other kind of life is what, as the verses above indicate, Jesus makes available to each of us. God wants to intermingle our ordinary, everyday lives with the divine life from above so that we seek it more deeply, pursue it more passionately, and receive it more abundantly. As we do this, we move beyond our inner deadness, our self-centeredness, and our emptiness into the fresh aliveness, other-centeredness, and fullness of life for which our hearts yearn. The invitation we receive is to seek and to find this eternal kind of life with God in the present moment.

Reimagining God's Good News

How does this *zoe* life take shape amid our everyday tasks of washing dishes, playing with the kids, going to work, dealing with family conflicts, paying our bills, staying healthy, building friendships, coping with illness, and grieving the loss of loved ones, as well as responding to the immense social struggles taking place on our streets for a more just and compassionate world? This critical question invites us to reimagine what God's good news looks like in the nitty-gritty of our ordinary, daily lives.

The best place to begin this work of reimagination is the earthly life of Jesus himself. After all, Jesus himself is the Kingdom of God on two legs. If we dig into Jesus' own words and deeds, we get a clear vision of what God's good news looks like in a human life. He is the fully alive one, who shows us what it means to embody God's life in a full, flesh-and-blood way.

Here are five inseparable threads from Jesus' life that give us a fuller glimpse of the abundant life he makes possible.

Intimacy with God

First, the *zoe* life is an *intimate* friendship with that boundless Mystery we call God.

As you know, Jesus repeatedly spoke to God in Aramaic as Abba, "my own dear Father." It was a form of address that combined closeness and wonder, affection and respect, trust and obedience. In the dark loneliness of the Gethsemane moment, Jesus prayed, "My Father, if it is possible, let this cup pass from me; yet not what I want but what you want" (Matthew 26:39).

We cannot make sense of Jesus' life without reference to his intimate union with a personal God who is always close, available, and accessible. Scholars today often refer to this intimacy that Jesus had with God as his "Abba experience"— a beautiful, inviting phrase that captures the profound closeness of his relationship with God.

The staggering good news is that today, Jesus wants us to share in this same oneness that he had with Abba. This is how Jesus himself expressed it: "All things have been handed over to me by my Father; and no one knows the Son except the Father, and no one knows the Father except the Son and anyone to whom the Son chooses to reveal him" (Matthew 11:27). The biblical word translated as "know" refers to the "heart knowledge" that comes when we interact intimately with another person. Here Jesus is saying he wants to make it possible for us to experience the same kind of intimate interaction—the same kind of knowing, loving, and trusting—that he had with his own Abba Father when he was on earth.

Imagine enjoying this "Abba experience" with God every day. We wake up in the morning knowing deep in our heart that we are the apple of God's eye. We are aware that God knows us by name, loves us as we are, and is closer than we can ever imagine. Throughout the day we are conscious of being enfolded in a Divine Mystery, actively and lovingly present in all things. We know that nothing can separate us from the glorious reality of God's everlasting love. We share honestly with God all our feelings and thoughts, whether they be angry or joyful, sad or happy, fearful or loving. We move from being polite with the Lord to sharing ourselves openly, truthfully, and vulnerably with God. We listen for any divine whisper there may be in our hearts. This is the intimate friendship with God into which Jesus gradually leads us within our daily lives.

I mentioned earlier that I invited Dallas Willard to come stay with us and teach in South Africa. Late one night, after Debbie and I had gone to bed, I heard someone speaking in our living room around midnight. I was jolted awake, thinking that we were being robbed. When I went to investigate, there was Dallas on his knees, in conversation with God. I was not used to intelligent professors participating in this kind of childlike friendship with God. For Dallas, however, this seemed to be a perfectly natural thing to do. It also whetted my own appetite to live with God in a more intimate, personal, and real way.

Would you not want to know God in this way too?

A Shared Life

Second, the *zoe* life is a *shared* life in which we come to discover our individual calling in God's family.

Not only did Jesus spend his life in a close community of friends but by his Spirit he also formed family-like communities of disciples who reached out to their surrounding world with the good news. Jesus knew that, for us to grow in intimacy with God, we would need each other.

We cannot journey far into the life that God offers without others. Our relationship with God is personal but never private. There is no solo spirituality in the New Testament. We need sisters and brothers who will encourage us, challenge us, and love us. Hence, when Jesus comes into our lives, he always comes with his arms around his family.

It is within this life together that we can explore the nature of our God-given, personal vocation. Writing to the communities of Christ followers in Ephesus, Paul encouraged them "to lead a life worthy of the calling to which you have been called" (Ephesians 4:1). On the one hand, this calling involves becoming the unique person God wants us to be, and on the other, it is about discerning how God wants us to serve others. Each of us is called to work out our calling in our own time, place, and season of life. In this way we play our part in making God's dream for our world more real. And as we do this, our own lives take on eternal significance and immeasurable meaning.

Imagine experiencing this shared life on a regular basis with kindred spirits along the way—gathering with young and old, women and men, single and married, black and white. We come from different economic backgrounds, hold contrasting political views, and have different numbers on the Enneagram. Every person gets an opportunity to speak about how their lives are going. No one tries to "fix" the other person, or to change them, or to correct them. Now and then, an open, honest, and respectful question gets asked. There are times of shared prayer, Scripture reading, and gathered silence. The focus is always on helping each other live into the personal calling that God has for us.

This kind of shared life really can happen!

Here is a glimpse of what it looks like. It is Tuesday night and Debbie and I have welcomed twelve thirtysomethings of various economic and personality types into our home. This is our third monthly meeting of our year-long journey together. As the group gathers in twos and threes around light eats and drinks, sounds of laughter and lighthearted conversations fill the air. After thirty minutes, we move from standing in the kitchen and dining room to sitting in our lounge, where the more structured part of our evening happens.

As usual we begin with a simple icebreaker to help us

connect in a light, yet significant way. Tonight, Debbie introduces it with an invitation, "Let us take a moment to share what the weather is like in our lives right now." For a few moments the group is silent, and then one by one each person gives us a peek of how they are doing. "It's cloudy, but the sun is beginning to shine through." "Gale force winds are blowing." "Things have been sunny recently." When we have finished, I am struck again by how we have learned to listen to one another with respect and attentiveness.

Then comes my turn to introduce the evening's open-ended question aimed at helping us bring our faith and life closer together. The question tonight focuses on seeking. "What are you looking for in your relationship with God?" For a few minutes we reflect quietly, make a few notes, and then when ready, we take our turn to offer our heart longings to one another. As each person shares, we have an opportunity to respond to their words. The ground rules are always made clear: No fixing, no advice, no judgment. After three meetings, everyone has had a chance to share about significant events from our very different lives. These bits of our life stories have moved us as a group beyond the superficial quite quickly.

After a closing time of prayer, the evening ends promptly at nine. On this Tuesday evening, I walk with Gail, a recently qualified corporate lawyer, to her car. She turns to me and says quietly, "Thank you for tonight. It's been great being here. I am slowly discovering the life that God wants me to live. I cannot talk about things like this anywhere else."

A Transformed Life

Third, the *zoe* life is a *transformed* life in which you and I are gradually changed into the compassionate likeness of God's unique image bearers.

Whenever Jesus met people, he accepted them unconditionally, but he did not leave them where they were. He challenged them to face the truth of their own lives, look at the logs in their own eyes, without judging or blaming others for what they were. He constantly affirmed those who lived gratefully, rather than taking things for granted. He wanted his followers to reflect the humility, trust, and sense of wonder of little children. Above all, he wanted them to love like he loved, to serve as he did, to have the joy he had, and to reflect the all-inclusive compassion of his own Abba Father.

We are also invited by Jesus into this journey of personal transformation. It is not a do-it-yourself job. Nor will it take place without effort on our part. As we open ourselves to the Spirit of Jesus, however, we gradually start to change inwardly. Over time we become more transparent, grateful, joyful, humble, trusting, loving, serving, compassionate human beings.

As this slow work of inner transformation takes place, through grace and through our own cooperation with the Holy Spirit, we begin to participate in the life that God makes available in Jesus Christ. We discover that we do not need to get stuck in destructive ways of thinking, living, and relating. Real inward change can happen.

Imagine our heart slowly changing like this over time. We sense it becoming more open toward others than ever before. No longer is it curved in on itself. We begin to become aware that the person next to us has an infinite, irreplaceable, and precious value in God's eyes, just as we have. There is a new gentleness with others, especially in moments of failure and struggle. We can let the other person be who they are without any need to change them. Our own suffering has helped us to see, hear, and feel the suffering of others, whether it is expressed or not. We know intuitively that we are joined with our neighbor, and with the whole creation, in an unbroken connection with God's heart.

I am sure you have seen this inner change in someone you know. Certainly, it has been an immense privilege for me, as a pastor, to witness God's transforming work in many people's lives.

Let me introduce you to Jim, a pastor in his mid-forties. I first met him when he made inquiries about doing the *Spiritual Exercises*. By his own admission, he was a driven, task-orientated, egocentric personality who liked to call the shots in his congregation. Sadly, this way of relating had infiltrated his marriage and brought about a painful crisis. He wanted to do the *Spiritual Exercises*, as he put it in his own words, "to open my life more widely to God and become a better person."

Over those ten months, as we met weekly, I watched the Spirit gradually change his heart. In the early months of the

Exercises, God gently revealed to him the depth of his self-centeredness and self-importance. As he meditated on Jesus' gospel life and death, his heart became porous to the compassion of God. He became more interested in the well-being of those around him, more responsive to their needs, and much freer from his attachments to work and outward success.

At the end of his Exercise journey, we met together with his wife to celebrate Communion and to reflect on our time together. When I asked his wife how she had witnessed her husband's engagement with God during his engagement with *Spiritual Exercises*, she smiled and said, "He is much more fun to live with."

A Powerful Life

Fourth, the *zoe* life is a *powerful* life in which God acts with us, both for the good of our lives and for the common good.

In his reflections on the life of Jesus, Luke writes about Jesus that "he was a good man, full of the Holy Spirit and of faith," who "went about doing good" (Acts 11:24, 10:38). Jesus, the fully human one, lived continually in the power of the Holy Spirit. Because of this, not only did he defeat the temptations of the evil one in his own life but he also freed those around him who were in bondage to evil. It is especially on the Cross that we witness the power of Jesus to overcome the power of evil. There evil unleashed its worst against the best person who walked this earth and was defeated by the power of the self-giving love of God in the crucified Jesus.

The same powerful resources of the Holy Spirit are freely offered to us. We, too, can overcome destructive temptations in the power of God's Spirit. In the words of the second step of the Alcoholics Anonymous twelve-step program, there is a Higher Power who can restore our lives to sanity.[1] Furthermore, when we do simple acts of goodness and kindness trusting in God, we will be amazed by what God's Spirit brings about through those actions. The extra blessing brought about by the Holy Spirit to those around us always exceeds what we can achieve with our own resources. The evil around us weakens, and the common good increases exponentially. This reminds us that life in "the kingdom of God depends not on talk but on power" (1 Corinthians 4:20).

Imagine being vitally connected with this inner-power resource as we face our daily temptations and trials. Knowing the availability of the Spirit's loving power, we can freely admit our powerlessness in those areas where we are constantly defeated. It could be in our struggles with addiction, or with our self-centeredness, or with our overwhelming fears and paralyzing anxieties, or with our unhelpful ways of thinking. After all, it is where we struggle the most that the Spirit makes us strong (2 Corinthians 12:10). Think, too, of receiving God's strength as we work for a more compassionate and just world, where we are. We will accomplish more than we ever could in our own strength.

I repeatedly witness God's power at work in twelve-step groups. Recovering addicts strongly believe there is a Higher Power who can empower us to live fuller and freer lives. They know firsthand that as they acknowledge their powerlessness regarding their addiction, they give access to a greater power who can restore their lives to sanity. This should be hopeful news for all of us. After all, we are all addicted or attached in one destructive way or another.

Some years ago, John H., who I mentioned at the beginning of this chapter, invited me to celebrate his thirtieth birthday of sobriety at his local Alcoholics Anonymous group with him. As is the usual custom on these occasions, he retold his own story of recovery. I watched the faces of those listening light up with hopeful possibilities for their broken lives as he spoke. "Take it from this recovering drunk," he said as he ended his testimony, "there really is hope for change."

The words he had spoken to that couple struggling with addiction were not merely theoretical. They had been birthed from his own lived experience.

It doesn't have to be this way!

An Indestructible Life

Last, the *zoe* life is an *indestructible* life that will never be snuffed out.

Jesus told his followers, "Whoever keeps my word will never see death" (John 8:51). Whatever else Jesus may have meant by this promise, he certainly was underlining the never-ending nature of our one life.

Unlike candles in the wind, the light of our lives will not be extinguished. Although we can be sure that the moment of physical death brings about many significant changes, our personal existence will continue. Our trusting obedience in Christ weaves all that we are, all that we do, and all that we have become into a glorious and eternal future. The resurrection life of Jesus gives us the assurance that God's life in us cannot be destroyed. We will live with and in God forever.

This indestructible life beyond the grave is not easy to imagine. I have been most helped by an analogy that I came across several years ago.

Think of the real you, the person you are becoming, as a message, and think of your body as the means of transmission. Like a message that remains the same, whether spoken in words, or flashed in Morse code, or typed in an email, so you and I continue to be the same "message," no matter what transmitter is used to transmit who we are. At death, our earthly transmitter returns to dust. But the message—that is, our unique personality—continues existing, only now it finds expression through a new God-given transmitter better suited to our new environment.

One of the most important things I learned from Dallas when I first met him involved a simple daily exercise that emphasized this indestructible life God gives us. He encouraged me to take time each day to look in the mirror and repeat aloud this sentence: "I am an unceasing spiritual being with an eternal destiny in God's great universe."[2]

I took his counsel seriously. Over the years I have memorized this sentence, shared it with my children, told my friends, whispered it to the dying, repeated it with my congregation. Now I am sharing it with you. I trust that its truth will help you, as it has helped me, to reimagine our eternal future with the living God.

The Painful Gap

To the limit of my own faith vision, I have sought to describe God's good news that Jesus proclaimed. It is, however, important for me to say that reimagining the life God gives does not mean that I have attained it. I constantly seek to catch up to the words I write. There is always a painful gap between the radiant, glorious, and shining life that I see in Jesus and my own life.

But I am slowly learning not to despair about this difference. I have learned over the years that God always meets us where we are, never gives up on us, and constantly encourages us to keep seeking the life Jesus makes possible for you and me. "Lord," I often pray, "I believe; help my unbelief" (Mark 9:24).

After forty years of working as a pastor and getting close to people, I have become convinced that this *zoe* life is our heart's deepest desire. We yearn for intimacy, belonging, significance, transformation, power, and eternity. This longing is written in capital letters onto the emptiness of our souls, the pain of our lives, the struggles of our relationships, and the strife of our shattered communities.

The good news is that amid our searching lives, our broken relationships, our battles with addiction, our desperate reaching out for something more, our fractured and hurting world, Jesus Christ reaches out to us with the compelling vision of another kind of life. He comes to us in his risen presence and says to each one of us,

> *It doesn't have to be this way. Another kind of life is available to you. You are invited into an intimate pilgrimage to the heart of my Abba Father, who loves you beyond your wildest imaginings. As you keep company with me, my sisters and brothers will become your new family. Over time I will reveal to you God's personal calling for your life. I will show you how you can partner with me in healing my Father's world. Along the way I will slowly transform you into the loving, compassionate, and generous person you were meant to be. My powerful Spirit will set you free from whatever enslaves you and will empower you to act on behalf of the common good. Above all, there is nothing that will ever separate you from the Father's love with which I love you. This is the divine vision I have for your one life on earth.*

The Necessity of Seeking

When we reimagine this *zoe* life offered to us by God, when our hearts are moved by the vision of living in the eternal Kingdom now, we begin to seek it. This life is not for passive observers, nor for uninvolved spectators. It is for those serious enough to ache for it, reach out for it, and turn in to it . . . and who are willing to give up whatever is necessary to obtain it. If we want to enter this life that God gives, you and I must become seekers.

I believe this is also what Ignatius would say to us from across the centuries.

His own seeking pilgrimage began when, as a soldier in a Spanish army, defending Pamplona in 1521 against the French troops, he was injured in battle. A cannonball shattered his legs. Inigo (he switched to the name Ignatius later) was taken by stretcher back to the family castle in Loyola. It was there, during the painful recuperation period, that he caught a surprise glimpse of what God could do with his life if he was willing to take following Jesus Christ seriously.

Lying in bed, after the most painful part of convalescence had passed, Ignatius asked for some romantic reading to pass the time. Let me say he was an idealistic daydreamer. He would spend time daydreaming about battles he would fight, fame he would achieve, and beautiful women he would court. Providentially, there were no love stories at hand to feed these fantasies. The only two books around were *Life of Christ* and *Lives of the Saints*. Probably these were the last things he wanted to read, but they introduced him to another kind of king, another kind of kingdom, and another kind of life. Something new and strange stirred within him, and he began to fantasize about following Christ like Francis of Assisi and Dominic did. He began to reimagine his life as it could be if he consciously lived with God.

For many weeks, Inigo alternated between these two sets of daydreams. Eventually he noticed something that would change his life and the lives of millions of others. The romantic dreams initially gave him a thrill and raised his spirits, but afterward they left him feeling flat, uninspired, and desolate. In contrast, his dreams of walking in the footsteps of Francis and Dominic left him feeling alive, eager, and energized. They were obviously more in tune with his truest longings than the other daydreams.

It was in noticing this difference between these two contrasting aftereffects that he concluded that God, through the deepest desires of his heart, was leading him toward a radically different kind of life. Rather than chasing fame and romance, he wanted now to seek the greater glory of God. He had become a God seeker.[3]

Certainly, there were times when his seeking looked extreme, silly, and over-the-top. Sometimes he got following Jesus painfully wrong, and yet at other times he got it wonderfully right. Thankfully, Ignatius kept reflecting on his seeking experiences, made notes about them, noticed what helped and what did not, and then put them together in the *Spiritual Exercises*.

Today, the life-changing consequences of his God-soaked life, and his training program for Christ followers, continues to bring huge blessing to seekers around the globe. They remind us of what God can do with a human being willing to seek him. Even if we get it wrong at times, as we surely will.

What Do You Seek Now?

Let us from move from Ignatius's sixteenth-century world back into ours. What are you seeking right now in your relationship with God? This was indeed the first question that Jesus asked in the New Testament.

John the Baptizer was standing with two of his disciples when Jesus walked by. John pointed toward him and called out, "Look . . . the Lamb of God!"

Intrigued by this description of Jesus, the two disciples began to follow Jesus. Suddenly he stopped, turned around, and asked them, "What are you looking for?" (John 1:35-39).

We need to take this question seriously. When we tell the Lord what we are seeking, it brings us into closer interaction with the one who is always interested in us and who wants to be in intimate relationship with us. Moreover, as those two disciples discovered for themselves, God often leads us on the next step of our faith journey through those deep heart desires we articulate.

This could be why, when I arrived late in the evening at a retreat center to do an eight-day, guided silent retreat two years ago, I found a note in my room from my retreat director. It read: "Dear Trevor, it is good to have you here. I will see you tomorrow morning at 9:05 a.m. in room 103. Before we meet, please spend some time listening to Jesus asking you, 'What do you want in your friendship with me?' Listen to what your heart longs for. We can speak about your response when we get together. Regards, Bill."

My retreat guide obviously knew Jesus' gospel question. He was also aware it is a question that comes from God at different stages throughout our life's journey. When we engage it, we again become a God seeker.

That is what happened for me on that retreat. Sitting down with Bill for the first time the next morning, I expressed my longing to him: "As I enter my seventies, I want to live much more freely and confidently in my friendship with the living Christ." For the next eight days, as I began to pray around that specific desire, the Spirit took me on a significant journey into both my own fears about the diminishments of aging and my need to trust God with the future.

SEEKING EXERCISE

To help clarify what you really seek right now in your relationship with God, you may want to reflect again on each of those five threads of the life God gives us which we looked at earlier. See which one gets your attention and evokes within you a sense of longing and attraction. Perhaps your interest is captured by deepening your intimacy with God, or having a stronger connection with God's family, or developing with others a clearer sense of your personal vocation, or experiencing a deeper transformation of your character, or receiving God's power to help you overcome a specific temptation, or discerning how best you can contribute to the common good, or growing your confidence

in God's never-ending love as you face your mortality.
Whatever you are seeking, write it down and talk with the
Lord about it. Then ask yourself: How can I follow the
longing of my heart with greater openness and trust?

As we become God seekers, we can be sure that what happened for Ignatius will also happen for you and me. God meets us in that seeking and leads us on pilgrimage into another kind of life, one step at a time.

The way God does this with each of us will always be unique. But one simple and profound truth remains the same: If we truly seek God with our whole heart, we will be found by God and experience the amazing life God gives. "When you search for me, you will find me; if you seek me with all your heart" (Jeremiah 29:13).

As we end this chapter, here is a simple prayer you can make your own:

Lord Jesus Christ, your good news has found
its way into my heart. Thank you for the divine
life that your own life, death, and resurrection
make possible for me today. I have caught a
glimpse of what this life looks like in your own

*life, and I yearn to know it for myself. Today
I turn toward you, trusting that this is your
vision for my life here on earth. As I learn
what it means to seek you and the life you give,
may your Spirit show me my next step.*

CHAPTER 3

CHANGING DIRECTION

When God, in Christ, says "Repent and believe the Good News,"
he is uttering an invitation, not a threat.

GERARD HUGHES, SJ

AT THE HEART OF THE GOOD NEWS is an open invitation to enter another kind of life. The risen Christ invites you and me to turn toward him and discover the life-giving difference he can make in our lives. This difference is the kind for which our restless and searching hearts long. As we saw in the previous chapter, the life that God wants to give us connects with our deepest longings for a better, fuller, and more meaningful life. *Zoe* life goes beyond all that we can dream and imagine for our one, unrepeatable life in this world.

The painful reality is that few within the church seem to find this different life. When I was at university preparing for the pastoral ministry, one of my best friends was studying to become a psychologist. We have remained in close contact over the years. The other day he said, "Trevor, after thirty-five years of counseling people who attend church regularly and those who don't, I have seen that there is little difference between the two groups. Church attendance doesn't seem to make too much difference to how people respond to the crises and challenges we all face. There doesn't seem to be greater compassion and love among those who identify as Christians than among those who don't."

I found my friend's conclusion challenging. Against the dark background of the consumerism, materialism, and narcissism that characterizes our surrounding culture, God's people are called to be signs of contradiction, our characters distinguishable by our capacity for self-giving love, speaking truth, and doing justice. When these changes happen within us, we change the world around us. Only then will the good news we share become credible in a cynical and critical age. It was the well-known atheist Friedrich Nietzsche who once remarked to a group of churchgoers, "I might believe in the Redeemer when his followers look more redeemed."

This could also be one of the main reasons why many younger people have left the church. They miss these distinguishable characteristics in our lives. Consider the recent changes in the religious landscape of the United States. In Pew Research telephone surveys conducted in 2018 and 2019, those who describe themselves as atheist, agnostic, or "nothing in particular" (also known as "religious nones") rose from 17 percent of the population in 2009 to 26 percent at the time of the surveys. About one in three millennials said that they had attended church around once or twice a month.[1] When asked why they choose not to identify with the church, one recurring reason was given: Christians lack compassion.[2]

It doesn't have to be this way. The good news declares that we can become different. We can discover another kind of life. This is the promise of the risen Christ given to those who genuinely become seekers. "Seek', he once said, "and you will find."

The Critical Necessity for Repentance

What I do know is that, if we become genuine God seekers, we will become radically different. Here is the reason why: Seeking God with our whole heart requires that we change direction. The biblical word for this redirection process is *repentance*.

Go back once more to those headlines of the opening sermon Jesus preached, which we explored in the previous chapter. "The time is fulfilled," he proclaimed, "and the kingdom of God has come near; repent, and believe the good news" (Mark 1:15). Repentance, supported by our faith, represents the part we play in the drama of our salvation. What, therefore, *is* repentance?

Metanoia, the original Greek word for repentance, means a complete change in our thinking. It is not about feeling miserable about our faults, or beating ourselves up for past wrongs, or putting ourselves down. It may involve feeling remorse for some of what we have done, but it is never about earning God's love, or deserving God's forgiveness, or meriting God's favor. True repentance involves something altogether different—a complete turnaround of our minds and lives, one that leads us in a new direction.

Remember the distinction Scripture makes between *bios* life and *zoe* life: the first kind is our physical, perishable, and created life; the second is the spiritual, imperishable, and eternal life that God wants to give us. When we turn toward Jesus and place our trust in him, we open ourselves up to receive this *zoe* life.

It is an eternal kind of life that we begin living then. The life of the Eternal One flows into and through us. We embrace a different way of living. Our lives become shaped by the gospel values of Jesus. We begin to see people as Jesus sees them. We start to love them, and ourselves, as he does. We can do things that before we could not do by ourselves, like blessing our enemies, forgiving those who have hurt us, and not letting the sun go down on our anger.

Consider this brief description of repentance: rerouting our lives, on the basis that there is another kind of life available to us in Christ, and taking practical steps to enter and grow in this divine life.

Could it be that Christ followers today fail to enter the life God wants to give because we have downplayed the importance of repentance? Perhaps, in reaction to a shame-based, guilt-focused, sin-obsessed understanding of repentance, much preaching and teaching today minimizes the role it should have in our spiritual pilgrimage. This is hugely unfortunate because repentance: (1) represents the doorway into the life God gives us; (2) keeps us on the pathway of walking with Jesus; and (3) opens our hearts to the overwhelming joy of God.

Let us drill down further into these three movements in the company of our friends Ignatius and Dallas Willard. Maybe the power of their words and lives can help us overcome our contemporary reluctance to explore the central place of repentance in our journey with God.

The Doorway of Repentance

If you saw a door with a sign labeled "Repentance" hanging on it, would you want to walk through it? And if you went through this doorway, what would you expect to find inside the room?

I have a hunch that these questions may evoke conflicting feelings in you. For many, *repentance* is a word that communicates a sense of threat. Perhaps, at one level, this threat is true. Repentance does threaten us when we build our lives around ourselves, putting ourselves first in all we do and pretending to be who we are not. It challenges us to find a new center for our lives, to give ourselves to others in love, and to honestly face who we really are.

Certainly, early in my Christian journey, I had a negative understanding of what repentance involved. Not so much for the above reasons but because of how I pictured repentance. The picture that usually came to mind was of a stern and unsmiling figure, dressed in a heavy overcoat, standing on the corner, holding a placard, threatening those passing by with the words "Repent, for the end is near." It wasn't a doorway through which I wanted to walk.

Yet we dare not abandon this word. The first invitation that Jesus gave when he began his preaching ministry was for his listeners to repent. From then onward, it was almost his constant invitation. Repentance is the doorway into that life which God gives and for which our heart most deeply longs. There is no other way to enter. Unless we walk through the door of repentance, we will not receive the *zoe* life that God gives.

Jesus was making available another kind of life, and he wanted his hearers to turn around, change their direction, and walk through this door. Or, as Dallas Willard explained, to repent is to "review your plans for living and base your life on this remarkable new opportunity."[3] So we need to stress that when Jesus called those around him to repent, he was inviting them to enter the fullness of life in which they would come to know that their lives had an eternal significance and an eternal destiny.

Recall Jesus' inaugural sermon once more. His hearers are urged to repent because the Kingdom of God has drawn near to them in him. In effect, he was saying to his listeners,

Change the direction of your lives. Rethink the way you are living, turn around, and enter the glorious new life God wants to give you. It goes

*beyond your wildest dreams and imaginings. It is
a life of ever-deepening intimacy with my Abba
Father and my family. As we journey together,
you will become the person you are designed to
be. You will discover how I want you to work
with me in healing this world. You will be slowly
transformed into a transparent, compassionate,
and caring human being. You will receive power
to defeat temptation within and to overcome evil
around you. You will never be separated from my
never-ending love for you and all creation.*

This is what Jesus invites us to. We accept this invitation when
we turn toward the generous Giver of this new kind of life.

This means turning away from whatever has previously
been at the center of our lives. We do not want to "play god"
any longer in our own lives or in the lives of those around
us. From this moment onward, we want to let God be God.
We intend now to leave behind whatever may sabotage and
rob us of the life that God gives. We aim to seek first the will
of God rather than our own. Rather than moving away from
God, we are now moving toward God. Or, to put it the other
way round, God is now drawing us into the *zoe* life that he
wants to give us. We have changed direction.

Ignatius's Doorway Moment

As we saw in the last chapter, after noticing the different experiences of his two sets of daydreams, Ignatius embraced his

deeper desire of following Christ. He decided to walk to the Holy Land as a pilgrim, to serve his new Lord there. Before he set off for Jerusalem, though, Ignatius made his way to a well-known Benedictine monastery high up a mountain at Montserrat, about four hundred miles away. There he demonstrated his change of direction in two significant ways.[4]

First, he came clean about his sinful past. For three days he reflected on his previous life, put together a written confession of his wrongdoing, and shared it with a wise French priest, who then gave him some counsel on how to grow in prayer. Ignatius knew that if he was going to start over with God, he would need to be radically honest with himself, with God, and with at least one other person. Although later he did keep rehearsing his sins in an unhealthy and unhelpful way, this honest moment of confession showed his seriousness about entering God's life through the door of repentance.

Second, Ignatius did something symbolic. He had arrived at the monastery dressed in the expensive clothes of a soldier, armed with his sword and dagger. To symbolize his decision to surrender himself wholeheartedly to God, he hung up his weapons at the altar, removed his fine attire, gave it away to a beggar, and dressed himself in a pilgrim robe. He wanted now to be bound irrevocably to God and to burn any bridge from his past life that could have swayed him from seeking first God and God's Kingdom.

We all need our own personal "Montserrat moment" if we are going to be serious about walking through the doorway of repentance. It will look different for each one of us. It could mean . . .

- writing a letter to Jesus expressing our desire to surrender ourselves to him;
- putting down on paper the specifics of past wrong-doing, reading it out in the presence of a trusted friend, and then burning it;
- making a public confession of faith within our community of faith; or perhaps
- keeping some visible symbol near us that reminds us of our decision to turn our life over to God.

Whatever we do, we must find our way of entering the life that God gives through the door of repentance that God's kindness has provided for us.

SEEKING EXERCISE

Recall your own "Montserrat" moment when you first walked through the doorway of repentance. Make a few notes of how it happened for you. Was it a sudden or gradual experience? Perhaps you have never walked through this doorway. If so, you may want to do so now. You could choose one of the ways above. Imagine turning toward Christ and entering another kind of life!

The Pathway of Repentance

Repentance is not a once-and-for-all experience. "Once converted, fully converted" is a deceptive slogan. We constantly discover new layers of self-centeredness and selfishness from which we need to turn. Our attachments to the idols of wealth, status, popularity, pleasure, power, being right, and success are much stronger than we usually think. Our collusion in the oppressive structures of society that rob others of their dignity and worth is both subtle and real. Thankfully, God is gentle with us and only gradually reveals the depth of our sinfulness. Hence, repentance is not only the doorway into the life God gives; it is also the pathway along which we need to walk throughout our lives.

This was my main discovery as I did the first part of the *Spiritual Exercises*. When I started to follow Christ as a teenager, I walked through the doorway of repentance. But I still needed to learn that repentance was the door *and* the pathway of the spiritual journey.

The reason is that our sinful behavior represents only the visible tip of the iceberg. Beneath our external actions of wrongdoing lie many hidden layers of disordered tendencies. These need to be brought into the light, confessed, and healed. This is a lifetime undertaking that we always need to keep up-to-date on.

Just yesterday, on my early morning run, my thoughts drifted to a person I respect. A video began playing in my head in which I started arguing with him about something he said. In this mental commentary that continued for at least two miles, I kept insisting on how wrong he was and how right I was. Even though I was surrounded by the glorious light of the sunrise, the conflict happening in my imagination kept me from enjoying it.

Eventually I realized that my attention had been hijacked by negative thoughts. As I continued running, I asked God to shed light on what was happening within me. "Lord," I prayed, "help me know what started this video." It wasn't long before another thought slipped gently into my awareness with startling clarity. *Trevor, it was your jealousy of your friend.*

First thing this morning, I took another step along the pathway of repentance. In the silence of my prayer time, I confessed and released this fresh revelation of jealousy into God's mercy. As I reflected on what may have brought it about, I was also able to recognize the arrogance from which it had sprung. Once again I yielded this part of my disordered heart to healing grace.

Ignatius's Pathway Wisdom

Two things from the *Spiritual Exercises* guide us wisely along this pathway of ongoing repentance into the life God gives.

First, the *Spiritual Exercises* invite us to ask God to show us the nature of our own inner disorder.

We are usually blind to the nature of the sin within us. We don't normally see what is going on beneath the exposed tip of the iceberg. Only the Lord can truly reveal the hidden waywardness of our hearts. We always need the gracious Heart Searcher to shine divine light into the depths of our inner darkness. We must, however, really want God to do this, for God is seldom pushy.

One way we can do this is to make the prayer of the psalmist our own:

> Search me, O God, and know my heart; test me and
> know my thoughts. See if there is any wicked way in
> me, and lead me in the way everlasting.
>
> PSALM 139:23-24

Let's be honest. When we think of asking God to reveal our sinful tendencies, it does sound a bit crazy. Who wants to pray like that?

When a friend comes up to us and says they want to point out something they don't like, it is a bit scary. If we are going to ask anyone to tell us the hard truth about ourselves, we need to know that we are deeply loved by that person. We need to be convinced that they will still accept us, believe in us, and be committed to our good, no matter what they know about our darkness and sin. This also holds true in our friendship with God.

We will ask God to reveal our sinful tendencies only when we know without a doubt that we are unconditionally loved by God. For this reason, before we start the *Spiritual Exercises*, it is critically important to have a strong sense of

God's personal, merciful, and creative love. We need to know deep down that right now, God earnestly wants to be our Divine Friend in mutual partnership with us. Then we are ready for God to begin revealing the hidden roots of our sin. After all, God lovingly sought us long before we ever began to seek God.

Second, the first part of the *Spiritual Exercises* invites us to take a few days to meditate on three scenarios: (1) the sin of some angels who rebelled against God; (2) the sin of Adam and Eve, who refused to obey God's word; and (3) the sin of an anonymous person who willfully rejected God's love throughout their life. As we reflect on these three scenarios and apply these reflections to our own lives, we begin to see how we share in this history of sin. The disordered and rebellious tendencies present in these case studies—vices like pride, arrogance, power, deception, selfishness, fear, lack of trust, jealousy, and blaming—also exist beneath the surface of our own lives. They poison our attitudes, contaminate our actions, and spoil our relationships more than we realize.

When I asked God during the *Spiritual Exercises* to reveal how these tendencies were at work in me, one of my most surprising revelations was to see the painful extent of my self-centeredness and selfishness. To be honest, I thought I lived a decent life, was a reasonably nice guy, and was mostly on par with those around me. There were no "big sins" tucked away from public view. As I pondered these three scenarios above, however, I realized that the sins of my heart had hurt others far more than the sins of my body. If

I was going to grow in the freedom of other-centered love, I would need to be liberated from the bondage of my self-centered heart.

As I was reminded, this will be a lifelong process.

Dallas Willard's Ongoing Repentance

One striking characteristic of Dallas's journey into the life God gives was his constant turning toward God. This becomes clear when we read the moving biography of his life, *Becoming Dallas Willard*.

He first walked through the doorway of repentance when he was nine years of age. At Sunday school he became convinced that Jesus Christ was the greatest person who had ever lived, and he wanted to be on his side. One Sunday evening, when the preacher offered the invitation for those present to give their lives to Jesus, Dallas went forward to the altar.

Much later in life he spoke about this doorway moment. "It was a remarkable experience. I remember how different the world looked as I walked home in the dark. The stars, the streetlights were so different, and I still have the impression that the world was really different. I felt at home in this new world. It felt like this is a good place to be; Christ is real."[5]

This was not the end of his journey of repentance and surrender. As his biographer, Gary Moon, observes, one of the benefits for Dallas of growing up in a revivalist tradition was its emphasis on the need for honest confession and repentance.

Quite movingly, as one reads of his early Christ-following days, we catch glimpses of his steps along the pathway of repentance. Some of these earlier steps included his awareness of how he had used words carelessly, coming to grips with twisted views around sexuality, and confessing his cheating in a critical university exam.

It was this experience of confession and repentance around his cheating that led Dallas, together with his marriage partner, Jane, into one of his most significant encounters with God.[6] At a revival meeting that took place on the evening of this confession, as the preacher laid hands on him, he was overcome by the real, living, and manifest presence of God. From that moment onward, he never felt that God was distant or had a problem hearing him.

But the pathway of repentance led Dallas way beyond the superficial level of his actions into the depths of his inner being. Later in his adult life he would admit that he had battled with vanity for many years. Often opportunities would come his way to show off his intellectual brilliance in public settings.

One fruit of his repentance in this regard was his resolve not to promote himself in any way. He would simply "do the best work [he could] by God's help."[7] This could be why he said to me, on his first visit to South Africa, "Don't ever look for a place to preach or teach. Just make sure that if anyone does ask you to do so, you have something to say."

It must be stressed that this emphasis on repentance does not mean we are constantly looking inward. Rather, exactly the opposite happens. We come alive to God as a living, active, and personal reality. Jesus becomes the most important person in our lives. We know the empowering resources of the invisible Kingdom within the ordinary visibilities of our day-to-day lives. Our hearts of stone change gradually into hearts of flesh—more attentive and responsive than ever before to the needs around us. We become different. We enter another kind of life, namely the *zoe* life that God gives to all those who turn toward him each day.

Right now, I am witnessing this inner change take place in a pastor I am giving the *Spiritual Exercises* to. He has just finished doing the first part of the journey, in which he has meditated on God's love and his own sinfulness.

When I asked him how he would describe his experience of the past few weeks, he said, "I have come to see how so many of my pastoral dreams were simply excuses to get my name in lights. The people in my congregation were there to help me get what I wanted. It has been hard facing up to this. But God is helping me see them very differently now. Each one of them is an important and valuable human being whom I am called to love and serve. I am asking Jesus to help me to do this."

Do you see how, when we walk along the pathway of repentance, our hearts get gradually turned toward God and those around us? As we honestly face our deeply embedded vices and confess them to God, the gift of God's compassion flows more strongly into us and through us to others.

SEEKING EXERCISE

*Join me today along the pathway of repentance. Daily
we experience the symptoms of our refusal to let the
compassionate God be the God of our lives. Whether we are
trying to control those around us, blowing up in anger because
we don't get our way, attempting to manage outcomes, or
withdrawing from others because they don't meet our needs,
reactions like these keep reminding us of our ongoing need
for continuing conversion. We must not get discouraged. We
simply ask God to bring to the surface what lies beneath
these reactions and consciously confess whatever it may
be. Repentance, we find out, becomes a way of life that
keeps us open to the wonders of God's transforming grace
and mercy. You may like to bring your repentance up-to-
date by asking God to be your Heart Searcher right now.*

The Joy of Repentance

You might be wondering right now whether this focus on
repentance can be healthy. Surely it will lead to us becoming
morbid. Are we not being too negative? Will it not rob us
of our sense of self-worth? What is the use of going over our
sin history?

Add to these wonderings the resistance that our contemporary culture has to any reference to sin, and these questions

get louder. This could account for some of the pushback I receive when I highlight the important place that repentance has in seeking the life that God gives us.

It is exactly the opposite. Genuine repentance opens us to great joy.

Dallas Willard would use this illustration: Imagine yourself invited by a dear friend to a special dinner. You arrive at the home of your host. As you walk down the passage, your host suddenly calls out, "Supper is ready in the dining room." As you turn through the doorway leading off the passage, you find yourself in a candlelit room, with the most beautifully laid-out table, with flowers and cutlery, in anticipation of the meal to come. You are so happy that you turned! Likewise, when we trust Jesus' announcement that "the kingdom of God is at hand," we turn into another kind of life, one that is overwhelmingly joyful.

Allow me to describe this multidimensional joy as best as I can. Imagine the joy of discovering that we are loved by a relentless, persistent, and passionate Lover. The joy of being unconditionally accepted as we are. The joy of receiving the liberating gift of divine forgiveness. The joy of beginning again with a fresh slate. The joy of feeling the weight of guilt and sin lifted from our shoulders. The joy of knowing that we are gradually being changed from the inside out into the compassionate image bearer you and I were meant to be.

Most of all, imagine the joy of coming to know personally that God "proves his love for us in that while we still were sinners Christ died for us" (Romans 5:8). Take a moment to savor this joy that we receive along the pathway of repentance and offer your gratitude to God.

I tasted this joy during the First Week of doing the *Spiritual Exercises*. Early in the journey, participants are invited to pray before the crucified Christ. They are to imagine Jesus on the cross, share with him whatever is on their mind, and ask him why he stooped down to come to earth and die on the cross for them. When I did this, I found these conversations overwhelmingly moving. As I looked at the face of the crucified Lord and shared the mess and muck of my heart, I experienced the loving gaze of his grace and mercy. My sin had not put me beyond the reach of his forgiveness. More than ever, I wanted to get to know this Jesus who loved me and all human beings this much and to serve him with the whole of my being for the rest of my life.

This is one good reason for wearing a cross or keeping one near us. Over the years I have given many small wooden crosses to those seeking the life that God gives. I ask them to put it someplace where they will see it often. Some keep it in their pocket, or hang it around their necks, or place it on their bedside table. After a while, I ask them about the effect this has had on their lives. I have learned that we don't need to understand everything that happened on the cross before we can experience the power of crucified love. Repeatedly, I was told that keeping the cross close by had brought a joyful sense of God's mercy and forgiveness.

Turning toward God does not only bring *us* joy; it also brings much joy to God. Remember the three parables Jesus shared with those called tax gatherers and sinners (Luke 15:1-32)? They were the shepherd who found his lost sheep, the woman who discovered her lost coin, and the father who rejoiced over the return of his runaway son. The common theme running through these stories is God's joy. Clearly, God loves to welcome home lost children, heal sin-sick hearts, and restore devastated lives. Repentance enables us to enter God's joy, to share the happiness that God has, and so to live more joyfully and freely.

Can you see now why, if our practice of repentance leads us toward a morbid preoccupation with ourselves, or to constantly beat ourselves up, we have somehow got it wrong? True repentance leads us in the opposite direction. It always frees us from self-preoccupation and restores our worth because we trust that God's goodness and love is always bigger than our sin.

Because we know that we are unconditionally accepted by God, we can now let go of our defensiveness. In fact, our capacity to take criticism, to evaluate it and to learn from it, grows. We are freer to laugh at ourselves, to see the humor in some of our mistakes, and to share in God's happy laughter.

Knowing We Are Beloved Sinners

The grace of the First Week of the *Spiritual Exercises* focuses on coming to know ourselves as *loved sinners*. As we have seen, both Ignatius and Dallas Willard knew this gospel truth about themselves. They arrived at this personal knowledge through their lifelong experience of repentance. They both knew that we never reach a stage before death where we no longer have a need to repent. In continually facing the deeper levels of their sinfulness, they came to know, in ever deeper ways, the loving goodness and compassionate tenderness of God. Furthermore, they both discovered that inner change was possible.

Many years ago, I conducted a weekend preaching mission in a congregation known for its liveliness and charismatic expression. Using the words of the Father to Jesus at his baptism, "You are my beloved son in whom I delight," I shared the good news that we are God's beloved. As the service ended, I offered an opportunity for those unsure about God's personal love for them to come forward. To my surprise, almost half those present, many of them churchgoers of long standing, came to the front of the church for prayer and counsel.

There are many possible reasons why some of us find it hard to know ourselves as God's beloved. Explanations may range from a lack of healthy attachment to our parents or conditional acceptance by our first caregivers to memories of painful abuse or present-day voices that undermine and ridicule to dehumanizing social conditions that mock the gospel's proclamation that every human creature is precious and loved by God. Tragedy, ongoing suffering, and painful disappointments can also make it hard to believe that God cares for us.

It is essential that, before we face our sinfulness, we come to know that we are God's beloved. It is highly unlikely that we will ask God to reveal the disorder of our lives if we are unsure about how God feels toward us. The ringing testimony of Christ followers throughout history, including Ignatius and Dallas, affirms that it is possible that these negative memories, voices, conditions, and experiences can be disempowered from having the final word about who we are. The good news is that you and I can come to know, both with our head and our heart, that we are loved by God, as we are.

This inner knowing goes beyond mere belief. It is an experiential assurance that we are God's beloved.

The Beloved Charter

How can we come to know that we are God's beloved in a more personal way? One of the best ways is to spend some time regularly meditating on God's personal love in Scripture, and to ask the Holy Spirit to make it more real for us.

Throughout the Bible there are many verses that underline the fact of our belovedness. When we put together what I like to call our personal Beloved Charter, it helps us see ourselves through the eyes of our loving God and begin to feel about ourselves the way God feels. With hearts and minds, we begin to see that God is recklessly in love with each one of us, that the divine Lover is interested in everything we do, and that God has unique purposes for our one life here on earth.[8]

To give you some idea of what a Beloved Charter could look like, here is the one that I wrote out for myself several years ago. It still speaks to me today.

Trevor, you are my beloved child in whom I delight.
You did not choose me; I chose you. I want you to be
my friend. I formed your inward parts and knitted you
together in your mother's womb. You are fearfully and
wonderfully made, made a little lower than the angels,
and crowned with glory and honor. You have been
created in Christ Jesus for good works, which I have
already prepared to be your way of life. When you pass
through the waters, I will be with you; and through the
rivers, they shall not overwhelm you; when you walk
through fire you shall not be burned, and the flame
shall not consume you.

You are precious in my sight, and honored, and I
love you. I know all your longings; your sighing is not
hidden from me. Nothing will ever be able to separate
you from my love for you in Christ Jesus, your Lord.
Abide in my love.

Coming to know ourselves as God's beloved sets the
foundation for life-changing repentance to take place in our
lives. Allowing words and images like the ones in my own
Beloved Charter to percolate within our hearts indicates
our willingness to let God be God in our lives, changes the
way we see ourselves, and helps us hear God telling us who
we are.

I am continually surprised by how the Spirit presses home
the message of a Beloved Charter into our hearts. Here is an
excerpt from an email of someone who spent a retreat day

putting together their personal Beloved Charter, meditating on its words, and speaking to God about it.

Thank you for your encouragement to put together my own personal Beloved Charter. When I imagined God speaking these words from deep within my own heart, it was quite difficult at first to believe that they could be true. I kept thinking that it was too good to be true. I have done many wrong things in my life, and it was hard to believe that God loved and accepted me unconditionally like these verses suggested. I kept feeling that I needed to do something to earn God's love. However, as the day progressed, there was a growing sense within that I am precious to God and embraced by his love. Almost every morning now, when looking into the mirror for the first time, I say to myself, "You are God's beloved." Whenever I do this, I smile.

SEEKING EXERCISE

Take some time to craft your own Beloved Charter. The very first word should be your own name so it is clearly addressed to you. Look up verses from Scripture that express the way God values our lives. Here are some Scriptures with which to begin:

Genesis 1:27

Psalm 8:1-9, 139:13-16

Song of Solomon 2:4

Isaiah 41:10-24, 49:15-16

Zephaniah 3:17

Matthew 6:25-34

Luke 12:6-7

John 1:12, 3:16, 15:15

Romans 5:6-8, 8:28, 32

2 Corinthians 12:9

Ephesians 2:4-10, 3:20

Hebrews 4:16

Circle those phrases that touch you deeply. If there are other verses that remind you of the way God sees you, write these down as well. Be sure to personalize the verses as being spoken directly to you. Do not use too many phrases, just those that you currently find the most compelling. Your whole charter should be no longer than six to eight sentences. If you are willing, set aside a few moments each day this coming week to be alone. Picture the risen Christ alongside you, speaking these words to you. Ask the Holy Spirit to press home the good news of your own belovedness.

Beginning Here and Now

God makes another kind of life available to us. Eternal living can begin right now, where we are. We enter this life through turning to Jesus and entrusting ourselves to him. We walk through the doorway of repentance, continue along the pathway of repentance, and experience the joy of knowing ourselves as loved sinners. As we change direction in this way, we are gradually transformed by God's love into the compassionate image bearers God wants us to be. We become different in a life-giving way.

SEEKING EXERCISE

As we end this chapter, I invite you to sit quietly with your hands placed on your lap. Curl up your fingers into tightly closed fists. Imagine that your tightly closed hands hold all your faults and flaws, all your visible and hidden sinfulness, all that weighs heavily on your conscience before God. Feel the tension build up from your hands and spread throughout your body.

Next, look at the cross where Jesus died for all. To express your response to God's offer of mercy and forgiveness, slowly open your hands—the one representing your desire to repent and the other your trust in the good news—and receive the gift God longs to give you.

As you end this exercise, you may like to pray with me:

Lord Jesus Christ, thank you for your grace-filled invitation to keep turning toward another kind of life. Please show me what gets in the way of my receiving the life you make possible. Without the light of your love shining into my life, I cannot see the true condition of my heart. Show me how you see me through your forgiving eyes and how you want me to change my ways. Reveal also to me the way you see the wayward ways of our church, our community, and our world. Help me to recognize how I contribute to this disorder, that I may learn to live more in tune with your dream for the entire universe. Thank you that I can ask for all this knowing that you always love me and want to help me change.

CHAPTER 4

DISCERNING OUR DEEPEST DESIRES

Our desires imply a condition of incompleteness because
they speak to us of what we are not or do not have.

PHILIP SHELDRAKE, SJ

FOR A FEW MOMENTS IMAGINE what your life would be like if you were living in harmony with the deepest desires of your heart. Think of the energy that would flow into whatever you were doing, as well as through you to those around you. In your mind's eye, see yourself motivated by what you feel strongly about, by what you most passionately value, by the powerful longings hidden within you.

Contrast this picture of yourself with what it is like when you just do what you are supposed to do, or what others expect, or what society dictates. Can you sense the difference? The contrast between living from the inside out rather than from the outside in?

This is a huge difference. Living in tune with our truest longings allows the life of God to stream into us and through us. We come alive to the sheer gift of our existence, to the wonder of our own uniqueness, and to our distinctive purpose in this big world. We find ourselves stretched beyond ourselves, bringing blessing to those around us, and connected with another kind of life, one much bigger than our own little lives. We become transmitters of beauty, truth, and goodness into the world around us. Intuitively, we know, *This is the life I am meant to live.*

When we are out of tune with what matters most to us, the opposite happens. The streams of God's compassion no longer flow in and through us as strongly as they could. We feel more dead than alive, and we drift aimlessly through life. Our lives shrivel up; we do not communicate life to others; and our faith seems bleak and barren. We wonder what creative difference we make in our world.

This contrast could be the reason why that wonderful slogan warns us, "Do not leave your longings unattended."

Our desires shape our lives, for better or for worse. They form us before we are aware of them.

Two years ago, I visited our twin granddaughters in New Zealand for the first time. For two weeks I watched their parents responding to their wants and desires. They would hold them when they cried, feed them when they were hungry, play with them when they were restless.

The desires of children invite our attention and response. Sometimes we try to meet these desires; at other times we refuse them. Later, as the children grow, they will become more conscious of their desires, and those desires will continue to mold them in creative and destructive ways, whether they find fulfilment or not.

Think, too, of how we are shaped by desires formed by our consumerist culture. Consider how we spend our money, even cash we don't have, accumulating more stuff. How are we persuaded to buy all these things? Each day bombards us with images and advertisements designed to entice us into desiring commodities we don't really need (yet we convince ourselves we must have). Without our conscious awareness, desires get formed within us that push us to accumulate more and more. These cravings sometimes become so insistent that they cover up the deeper longings of our heart.

Given how desires shape our lives, one would think that careful attention would be given to our desires in our churches. Yet I have seldom met anyone brought up in the church who was taught about their importance. If mention was ever made of them, it was usually negative.

Certainly, this was true for me in the church circles I moved in as a young adult. My wants were to be put aside if I wanted to do what God wanted. They were to be viewed with suspicion, to be subdued, to be crucified. What God willed for my life, it was assumed, would always be different from what I wanted. If I desired something, it was probably not what God wanted me to have.

What has your experience been in the church regarding the place of desire in the spiritual journey?

I want to suggest that our desires do not always oppose God's will. Instead, they are a vitally important dimension of our humanity and of our life with God. While not all of them are authentic expressions of who we truly are, discerning the deeper desires of our heart can lead us toward becoming who God wants us to be and doing what God wants us to do. When we become more open to our desires, and allow them to guide us, we find the life God wants to give us.

Desire in Our Life with God

As we affirm the important place that our desires have in our walk with God, two introductory comments set the scene for our further explorations into this theme. They represent the two sides of the same coin of desire. We need to continually hold them together in our conversations about the relationship between our desires and what God desires. When it comes to the task of discovering our deepest desires, these two aspects of desire encourage us to be thoughtful, reflective, and discerning.

The Gift of Desire

Desire is a deep, vital, and integral part of what it means to be human. God has created us with immeasurable desires. We have material desires for shelter, clothing, and cars. We have physical desires for food, sex, and drink. We have vocational desires to do well, to succeed, to stretch ourselves. We have relational desires for connection, intimacy, and belonging. The list goes on and on. We wouldn't be human without these desires.

As we have already seen, we enter this world with desires. We are desiring creatures. We have been gifted with desire. These desires bring vitality, energy, and joy into our lives. Indeed, they shape profoundly the person we become.

I am married to Debbie, who has an intense desire for beauty. She comes alive as she works in the garden, tends her roses, waters the shrubs, and arranges flowers in each of our rooms. When her mood is heavy, or when she comes home tired from a day's teaching, a few moments of garden creativity reenergize her like few other activities can. Even when visiting friends, it is not long before she is in their garden, plotting new expressions of beauty with them. Living in tune with her longing for beauty opens her heart to receive the life God gives.

We should not be surprised by our capacity for desire. We are created in the image of the God who relates passionately to each one of us. Our very existence expresses God's desire for friendship and partnership with us. God did not create us because God needed us. God created us because God wanted us to be here. You and I, it could be said, are expressions of God's desire.

Not only did God create us, but God loved us so much that God came into this world in Jesus to save it. Jesus' parables in Luke 15 (the lost sheep, the lost coin, and the prodigal son) are sometimes called "parables of desire" because they remind us just how much God yearns for intimate connection with us. Indeed, God's desire for us is the springboard of our own desire for God.

Before we move on, stop reading for a moment and ponder this startling thought: *God desires you.*

Sometimes, first thing in the morning, when I look at my reflection in the mirror, I remind myself of this astounding truth. I say something like this: "Trevor, God wants you to be here. God likes you and right now passionately desires to live in intimate friendship with you."

Even though I long to be desired like this, it is not always easy to accept this astonishing good news. But when with simple trust I let God's desire touch my heart, the longing to give myself to God much more generously, wholeheartedly, and freely becomes stronger.

SEEKING EXERCISE

Right now, I invite you to put down this book and go to where you can see a reflection of yourself. Remind yourself that you are someone to whom God is immensely attracted. See yourself through the divine gaze.

Consider that in this present moment, God desires you and longs to live in union with you. God wants you to be here, in this place, now. God seeks you more than you seek God!

As you reflect on God's passionate desire to live in friendship with you, what do you find yourself thinking and feeling? Is there any resistance to God's attraction to you? Tell God about this as honestly as

*you can and ask for the grace to journey beyond this
ambivalence. Remember, it is God's desiring of us that
releases our deepest and most authentic desires.*

The Distortion of Desire

Although desire is a part of our humanity, our desires can get distorted. They can become dark, destructive, and dangerous. They can lead us, not toward life, but toward death. I am not just thinking about our desires for dark chocolate and sweet cake. I have in mind our desires for money, for power, for reputation, for status, for sex.

Unsurprisingly, we come across strong language in the Bible warning us about certain desires. Peter, writing to the early followers of Christ, encourages them: "As aliens and exiles . . . abstain from the desires of the flesh that wage war against the soul" (1 Peter 2:11). Primarily, these sorts of desires are egocentric. The image of these desires waging war against our soul is a chilling one—they can tear our lives apart.

Think for a moment of how misdirected, untamed, and unchecked desire can lead toward addictive tendencies. Addiction "means being so completely possessed that one is enslaved, deprived of inner freedom, and ultimately of personal integrity."[1] We can become addicted to a substance or an activity. Substance abuse usually involves a physical dependence on anything that induces a change in mood, such as alcohol, drugs, caffeine, or even chocolate. More acceptable, yet even more dangerous to our souls, are the many ways we can get hooked on activities such as making money, gaming, online chats, social media, work, earning praise, keeping up appearances, or even religious activities. Both forms of addiction have one thing in common: distorted desire.

This distortion of desire gives desire a bad name. A reasonable desire to make money becomes greed. A healthy appetite degenerates into gluttony. The yearning for intimacy develops into lust. The search for significance turns into the pursuit of success at all costs. The drive to succeed backslides into workaholism. The desire to help others slips into people pleasing. The enjoyment of a glass of wine collapses into alcoholism. In reaction to these examples of desire gone wrong, many become ambivalent about the role that desire has in our spiritual journey. We may even think that being truly spiritual means ignoring or denying all personal desires.

Yet suppressing all our desires, our longings, and our wants is unhelpful. Our journey into another kind of life gets derailed when we ignore them. Since they are both a gift and a danger, we need wisdom about how to engage our desires.

While clearly signaling the dangers of disordered desire, Ignatius and Dallas offer us helpful guidance. Both knew that paying attention to what we want is vitally important for an authentic spirituality. They were aware of how our desires can trip us up, yet they also underlined desires' importance for our seeking journey.

Wisdom from Our Two Companions

Intriguingly, Dallas and Ignatius echo each other in the wisdom they offer us. They would both encourage us to ask for what we most genuinely want in our friendship with God.

I wonder if you ever received this encouragement from your teachers in the faith. The message many of us got was the opposite. It went something like this: *If you want something, you can be pretty sure it is not what God wants for your life. We must deny what we want to do and do what God wants instead. To follow our own desires indicates personal willfulness, selfishness, and disobedience to the will of God.*

Certainly, this was the emphasis of the teaching I got in relation to my own desires and wants. How do we need to reorient our thinking about desire?

Praying Our Desires

There is some truth in the negative message about desire. Jesus made it clear that our priority is to seek first the reign of God. Our wants can draw us away from this central gospel commitment.

Ignatius was aware of this possibility of getting distracted. At the beginning of the *Spiritual Exercises*, he makes it clear that they are designed to help us bring "an order of values into our lives, so that we make no choice or decisions because we have been influenced by some disordered attachment or love."[2] Notice that, for Ignatius, desires themselves are not the problem; *disordered* desires are. The problem comes when what we want becomes our god. It is Ignatius's hope that God will free us from these idolatrous attachments so that we may discover what our hearts truly desire.

There is, however, also a positive emphasis on desire in the *Spiritual Exercises*. Throughout them, at the beginning of every period of prayer, we are encouraged to ask God our Lord for what we want and desire. This instruction reveals what may have been in Ignatius's mind when it comes to the relationship between God's will and our desires. He didn't see them as necessarily opposed to each other. He believed that, when we are in touch with our deepest desires, we would be in touch with our hearts, where God dwells. He trusted that our most authentic and genuine desires would lead us toward communion with God and into the life that God gives. Centuries ago, the teacher in Ecclesiastes put it clearly like this: "God . . . has also placed eternity in [our] hearts" (Ecclesiastes 3:11, CEB).

In the various stages of the *Spiritual Exercises*, Ignatius states what our desire is to be.

- In the first stage, known as the First Week, the desire is to know how deeply we are loved by God in spite of our sinfulness.
- In the Second Week, when we meditate on the events of the life and ministry of Jesus, we desire to know Jesus more intimately so we can love him more deeply and follow him more closely.
- In the Third Week, as we journey with Jesus toward the cross, the desire is to be with him in his suffering.

- In the Fourth Week, we ask to share in the joy of the risen Christ and to know his consolation in our lives.

Each of these desires expresses an intense longing for the Lord to reveal himself to us so that our friendship with him may deepen and grow.

On the face of it, it looks as though Ignatius could be saying, "Here is what you should desire at each stage of the journey, so put aside your own desires and crank up some desire in this direction." The Ignatian scholar and spiritual director William Barry, SJ, warns us against this interpretation and approach. Instead, he suggests, Ignatius gave his instructions to us to help us recognize what we most truly want and desire in our relationship with God. The emphasis always is on expressing our most authentic desires. These desires change as our friendship with God deepens and goes through different stages. After all, what we really desire is a diagnosis of where we are in our friendship with God.[3]

Sometimes we lack the desire for what we know we should desire as Christ followers. Here is one example: We hold resentment toward someone who has hurt us. We realize that the bitterness pours poison into our soul. We know that Jesus wants us to forgive. We are aware that our lack of forgiveness impedes our joy and peace. Yet we have no desire whatsoever in our heart to forgive this person. What is the honest way forward in a situation like this? What does authentic prayer look like? How do we desire what we know God would want us to desire?

If Ignatius were our spiritual director, he would gently ask us, "Do you have the desire for this desire? Even if you don't want to forgive, do you want to want to go on the journey toward forgiveness? Would you like to become the kind of person who lives beyond bitterness and resentment? Would you like to live more freely and lightly in your relationships? Would you like to have a heart of flesh rather than a heart of stone?"

As we share with God our honest feelings about not wanting what we know God wants, God meets us where we are. Turning to God in our reality of conflicting desires, and asking for the desire to have the desire, opens the door for the Spirit to lead us forward.

Expressing Our Wants

Like Ignatius, Dallas was acutely aware of the light and dark sides of desire.

On the one hand, he warned about becoming enslaved to distorted desires. The motto of those who become willing slaves to their feelings is "I want what I want when I want it." Dallas would have agreed with Ignatius that we desperately need to be freed from our disordered attachments in order to enter the life God gives us. In his own haunting words, he believed it was possible to become so locked into self-obsession and self-worship that we could reach a place where we *cannot want God*.[4]

On the other hand, Dallas was a man of great desire. One of the main reasons he pursued studies in psychology and philosophy, he said, "was my desire to understand the things of the soul."⁵ He invested his life in these studies. In one sweet letter to his wife, Jane, at a marriage-encounter weekend, under the theme of "Why I want to go on living," he reflected on his experiences of beauty and books and love, and wrote movingly about the strength of his desire to live and to love. "I cannot *feel* the desire not to live, or not desiring to live."⁶ Underneath everything was his heart's constant longing to love God, to live faithfully in God's Kingdom, and to bless those around him.

His visits to South Africa were marked by many lengthy personal conversations. He often emphasized the importance of clarifying what we want.

Three conversational snippets recorded in my journal stand out for me. The first happened near Homestead Dam, in my hometown of Benoni. While we walked along the pathway, surrounded by ducks, I spoke about my fear of death, the journey of growing older, and the goals I still hoped to accomplish.

Out of the blue, Dallas stopped, turned to me, and asked, "How many years do you still want to live?"

That question, with its emphasis on the word "want," literally stopped me in my tracks. I had never thought about my life in those precise terms.

When I shared my hopes for the future, he suggested that I share them with the Lord in my prayer. "It is important that you tell the Lord very honestly what you want. While you will certainly not always get what you want, and your 'want-er' may also need to undergo radical transformation, the Lord can only meet and bless you where you are. He will meet you where you are and lead you on from there to where he wants you to go."

The second conversation revolved around challenges I was facing at that time, of being father to my two children growing into young adulthood. I was sharing my tension between setting boundaries for them and setting them free to make their own choices.

Dallas leaned strongly in the latter direction. These were his words as I recalled them afterward in my journal: "Let Joni and Mark begin to make their decisions around what they really want. Help them to know that, while they are free to choose whatever they want, they are not free to choose the consequences." I have shared that wisdom with many other parents.

The third conversation revolved around my experience of God's silence, when I sought guidance on a possible change in vocational direction. None was forthcoming. Heaven seemed to be silent.

When I shared this with Dallas, he said simply, "I am reasonably sure that if God had anything in mind, he would have let you know by now. Maybe God wants you to go ahead and do what you really want to do. It is unlikely that God plays games of hide-and-seek when we ask for guidance."

No one before had ever made this link for me between God's will and my will, between what God wanted and what I wanted, between God's desires and my desires. I realized that following God's will would sometimes mean that God wants me to decide what I *want* to do.

This wisdom from Ignatius and Dallas reminds us that our deepest desires really do matter. They matter because God intends us to live as adult children in the Kingdom. As Dallas repeatedly emphasized, our unique eternal calling as human beings, in partnership with God, is to reign with him, now and forever.[7] If God must tell us every time what to do, we will remain immature. Hence God sometimes leaves us with the responsibility to discern our truest desires and decide which way we want to go.

The desires of our heart also matter because they give us hints of our personal calling. They guide us toward what we are called to be, to live, and to do. Our responsibility is to choose between those life-giving desires that lead us to become the person God wants us to be and those disordered ones that take us in the opposite direction.

Above all, our deepest desires matter because through them God leads us into the life that God wants to give us. Formed in our heart by the Spirit, these hidden longings echo what God longs for within our own unique circumstances. As we learn to discern and respond to them, the consequences are transformative. We move toward greater intimacy with God and others. We become different in a compassionate and loving way. We receive strength from a power source beyond ourselves. We realize that nothing, not even death, can separate us from God's love. We discover *zoe* life in the here and now.

Can you see why discerning our desires becomes essential? To this practical task we now turn.

A Toolkit for Discerning Desires

Let us look at the Gospel encounter between Jesus and the blind Bartimaeus (Mark 10:46-52).

Bartimaeus was seated by the side of the road when Jesus and his disciples passed by. When he heard that Jesus was near, Bartimaeus shouted out, "Son of David, have mercy on me."

The crowd told him to be quiet, but he was insistent in his desire and again cried out to Jesus.

Finally, Jesus called him and asked, "What do you want me to do for you?" It is a question that has several layers of meaning that are relevant for us as we build a toolkit for discerning our desires. Let me tease some of these out.

Noticing Our Desires

Jesus asked Bartimaeus, "What do you want me to do for you?" Imagine how this question must have floored him. Surely Jesus would have known what the man wanted! Jesus, however, wanted Bartimaeus to get in touch with what he desired. What did Bartimaeus want more than anything else in the world?

Jesus' question invites us into a similar exploration. Jesus wants us to pause, listen to our heart, and recognize what we really want.

Many of us avoid this inward journey. We make excuses. We say we're too busy, or it's a waste of time, or it's too painful, or it will lead to selfishness, or we think that reasoning offers us a better guide to our lives. The list goes on. Some of us have also had our capacity for desire scarred by painful disappointment.

Whatever the reason may be, the result is always the same. We miss the opportunity to notice the desires of our heart and hear what God may be saying through them.

The consequences are sad. We rob ourselves of living an energetic life of depth and wonder and passion. We miss out on an intimate connection with God and with others. Perhaps the gravest consequence of not being aware of our different desires is that we cannot sift through them to see which come from God and which don't. We get captured by our lesser desires rather than following the greater ones. We can only see which desires are life-giving when we stop to reflect on and notice what they are. This means we must take this question from Jesus seriously, stop in our busy lives, and give attention to our longings and yearnings.

As a pastor, I have learned from Ignatius and Dallas to sometimes ask others, "What do you really want?" These conversations usually take us beneath the surface.

I'm reminded of a forty-something-year-old man, a nominal churchgoer, with whom I have been having lunch a few times each year. Over the years, I had built a level of trust where I could risk some personal questions.

One lunchtime, I asked him what he most wanted as he faced the second stage of his life.

"Well, I guess, I just want to be happy," he said.

Knowing that he was happily married and had a good job, I wondered aloud, "What do you think would bring you the happiness you want?"

"I am not really sure," he responded. "Something is missing from my life, and I can't really put my finger on what it is."

As we explored what could be missing, he used a poignant phrase that I have heard a few times. Wistfully, he said quietly, "There must be something more."

We sat in silence for a moment. Then he added with a smile, "That's what I am looking for! I am looking for the 'something more.' Where do I find that?"

We are still in conversation. My friend is building a toolkit for discerning his "something more." He is noticing the desires of his heart. It still feels strange, unfamiliar, and even a little uncomfortable for him. He struggles at times to put into words what he longs for.

I can understand this. Even though we acknowledge how important it is to respond to Jesus' question, finding words for what we want is not a simple matter. The language of the heart takes time to learn. When we do learn, though, our conversation with God extends to a deeper level.

This is happening for my friend. He is talking with God about matters that he has never spoken about before. He is also (I believe) on the edge of discovering another kind of life.

Sifting Our Desires

When Jesus asked Bartimaeus what he wanted, he was inviting him to name what he wanted most of all. What do you want, Bartimaeus? Do you really want to give up begging for a living? Do you honestly want another kind of life? Do you genuinely want to become responsible for the life you have? There were many possible answers. Bartimaeus's response was "Let me see again." He wanted what only Jesus could give him. This was the deepest desire of his heart. His intensely focused desire brought him both the healing and the new life he wanted.

It is not always easy to discover what we desire the most. Just try answering that question immediately! One reason it is hard is because when we are asked what we want, usually many desires come to mind. It is easier to name those that are more superficial than the deeper ones. We may write down immediately things like

- "I want to lose weight."
- "I want to stop smoking."
- "I want a new car."
- "I would like a different job."
- "I want more money."

There is nothing wrong with these surface-level responses. But if we stop with these, they keep us from looking deeper.

We must not write off these more superficial desires. We come to know our deepest desire by sifting through our surface desires. They are necessary signposts on a journey toward what is most true and genuine within us. They are not irrelevant to finding out what our deeper desires are. Sometimes the only way we can identify what desires lie at the core of our being is to begin with those at the uppermost of our minds and then follow them downward toward the longings that lie beneath. Discernment involves noticing our many desires, sifting through them, and distinguishing the deeper ones from the more superficial ones.

It is also hard to identify what we want most when we get pulled in different directions by contradictory desires.

One strong desire of mine is exploring with others in week-long retreat settings what it means to live in a friendship with God today. It brings me great joy and profound fulfillment to do this whenever I'm invited to do so. But doing this often necessitates time away from home. I also want to spend time with Debbie, to relax with her as much as possible, and to enjoy our life together. We are both getting older, and I know that our time together is limited. It is not always easy to sift through these conflicting desires and to know which one I need to follow in the moment.

Facing incompatible desires raises the critical question: What is the most fundamental desire of my heart that can guide me through these tensions and conflicts in my life? Sifting through our responses to this question until we begin to find some clarity about what we most want is what discerning our deepest desires is all about.

Asking for What We Desire

Recall our Gospel story one last time. Jesus was really interested in what Bartimaeus wanted. "What do you want me to do for you?" It was an honest question.

Bartimaeus took the question seriously too. He didn't assume that Jesus knew. He asked Jesus for what he wanted. "My teacher," he answered, "let me see again."

Bartimaeus's asking led to him getting his sight back and entering more fully into the life God gives us. Notice how the story of his healing ends not only with him been able to see but also with him following Jesus "on the way," into another kind of life (Mark 10:52).

Here we come to the third ingredient necessary for our discernment toolkit: Asking for what we most desire.

As we have already noted, both Ignatius and Dallas stressed the importance of asking for what we want in our friendship with God. We share with the Lord our real desires, wants, and longings, and we give God time to respond.

Remember, God meets us where we are, in the midst of what we want, and leads us on from there. Any relationship that is moving toward intimacy requires time and patience and this kind of honest, vulnerable asking. Sometimes it will become clear that what we ask is way off the mark and requires radical reshaping. We do not, however, give up on asking. "Asking," Charles Spurgeon maintained, "is the rule of the kingdom."[8]

You may wonder why God wants us to ask for what we want. Here is an analogy from Gerard Hughes that helps me:

Imagine a couple getting married. They have written their own vows for the wedding service. The groom says to the bride, "You are my heart's delight, and I love you with all my being. I will love you for richer and for poorer, in sickness and in health, until death parts us. However, you must understand that from this moment on, I have no interest at all in what you desire or want. From now on, your happiness consists solely in submitting yourself to my will, with complete dedication and with no thought for your own."

After the groom says this to the bride, the minister asks the woman, "Will you take this man as your husband?"[9]

How do you think the bride will respond? Not very well, I think.

Many people believe that God is like this bridegroom in that scenario. Yet our Gospel story reveals a very different picture of God. The God we meet in Jesus is concerned and interested in our desires. God would like us to bring them in prayer.

Jesus' response to Bartimaeus's request encourages us to see that God really cares about we ask for. This does not mean that we always get what we want. Not all our desires express the truest longings of our hearts. Some are quite self-centered and superficial. If God granted them, we would never discover the truer desires of our heart. Selfish desires can push us in destructive directions. If they were expressed, they would cause great pain. But God meets us where we are, no matter what our desires are, and then gives us the light we need to sort out which are deepest.

Attending to Our Deepest Desire

As I reflect on the countless conversations I have shared with women and men, I have become convinced of one thing: "There is in each of us, at the core of our being, a burning desire that is insatiable, irrepressible and unfathomable, a sense of incompleteness."[10] This is our heart's longing for God and the life that God gives.

Attending to this burning desire launches us into the transforming pilgrimage of the seeker toward another kind of life. As my spiritual director said to me many years ago, "Trevor, your longing for God is your bus ticket home."

Now, I don't think it is enough for me to say to you, "Your deepest desire is for God, and you must attend to it." Telling people to desire God has little or no actual effect. Rather, as we pay attention to our many different desires and sift through them carefully, God tenderly leads us beneath our surface-level desires to what our heart most truly yearns for: firsthand relationship with that boundless, creative, and loving Mystery whom we call God.

Or we could acknowledge, as some already have, that there is a hole in our hearts that only God can fill. We may have tried to fill this hole with other relationships and activities. We focus our longings on another person, or on career goals, or on possessions, or on personal achievements, hoping that these things may fill the hole. While there may be nothing wrong with these things in themselves, none of them meet the deepest desire of our heart. We know only too well that when we take the time to reflect on our own experiences of feeling incomplete, only communion with God, and the life God gives, can begin to fill this hole.

Another way to come closer to what we desire most is to pay attention to our experiences of wonder. We watch a sunrise starting with a gray light that turns brown, then blue, then gold, then redder and redder, and we marvel at a day's beginning. We hold in our arms a newly born baby, and we are overcome by the fragile miracle of life. We enjoy a moment of close intimacy with a loved one and are filled with overwhelming gratitude. We stare at the simple "thereness" of a huge mountain and feel our smallness and creatureliness.

These moments, and others like them, put us a little more in touch with our deeper longings. If we nurture them, they could awaken us to our longing for God that lies at the core of our being.

Whatever may help us to attend to our longing for God, we need to realize that this desire itself is God's activity within us. God lives on the inside of our longing for communion with God. We do not manufacture or create our God-directed desires. Nor are we trying to get God interested in us through the intensity of our desiring. Every time we reach out for the life that God gives, it echoes God's seeking love streaming toward us. God is constantly attracting us into friendship through the desires and longings of our heart. Our desiring God is a pale reflection of God's desire for you and me.

SEEKING EXERCISE

Take some time to practice with this toolkit.

*Begin by noticing your desires. Ask yourself: What do
I want? What are the desires of my heart? Find some
paper and scribble down whatever comes to mind.
Be as honest as you can. It is for your eyes only.*

*When you have your list completed, begin the sifting process.
As you reflect on what you have written, ask yourself: "What
are my surface desires and what are my deeper desires?
Notice those desires that conflict with each other.*

*Imagine the risen Christ asking you, "What do you want
me to do for you?" Let the question lead you into an
unhurried conversation with the Lord about your desires.*

*Finally, attend to your deepest desire, the one that lies
beneath all the others, the one that expresses most deeply
your longing for God. Keep wondering about this root
desire, the one from which all the others seem to come.*

———————

Are you willing to join me in the journey of embracing our
deepest desire? If you are, you can say something like this
to God:

Come and fill the hole in my heart. I want to come to know you, and to love you, and to follow you. I want to share your desires for my life and the world. Please shape all my desires so they may echo yours. Help me to learn from those who have gone before me, people like Ignatius and Dallas, who have sought to shape their lives according to your desires. Above all, help me to make those daily choices that will enable me to live more in tune with your dream for my life and our world, for this is my deepest desire.

CHAPTER 5

EXPLORING LIFE'S GREATEST OPPORTUNITY

Jesus . . . is, simply, the brightest spot in the human scene.

DALLAS WILLARD

"WHAT GOD HAS JOINED TOGETHER, let no person put asunder." Those challenging words remind us that we must seek to keep together what God has brought together. In this chapter we will see that these words apply not only to those who enter the covenant of marriage. They speak also to that critical relationship between the life God wants to give us and the call to discipleship. We cannot have one without the other.

There is a great need to be clear about this.

One the one hand, as we saw in chapter 2, Jesus proclaimed the availability of another kind of life. It is a life marked by growing intimacy with the God whom Jesus called

Abba, shared with others in community in which we discern our personal calling, characterized by our gradual inner transformation into God's compassionate family likeness, empowered by God's Spirit to overcome evil both within and around us, and most wonderfully of all, an indestructible life in which nothing can separate us from God's enduring love toward us in Christ Jesus. This is the priceless gospel offer that Christ makes available to you and me.

On the other hand, we enter this *zoe* life when we turn toward Jesus, place our trust in him, and become his disciple. Unless we become his disciple, we will not know the marvelous freshness of the life God gives. This availability of another kind of life and the call to discipleship go together. Hence Jesus, immediately after he announced his good news of the availability of God's Kingdom, invited Simon and his brother Andrew to become his disciples. "Follow me," he said to them, "and I will make you fish for people" (Mark 1:17). We seek the life God gives as we embark on this journey of discipleship.

Discipleship, understood like this, is an integral part of Jesus' good news. We need to grasp this, because sometimes we see discipleship as the hard part of Jesus' message.

In my early twenties I read my first serious theological work. It was *The Cost of Discipleship* by the German pastor Dietrich Bonhoeffer. Few books have affected me as powerfully in my understanding of what it means to follow Jesus. But the one possible downside of the word *Cost* in the book's title is that it could lead the reader to believe that becoming a disciple of Jesus robs us of the possibilities of living lightly and freely, allowing discipleship to be understood as a heavy burden we must carry if we want to know the life God gives.

While Jesus' first disciples certainly faced some difficult, demanding, and dangerous challenges, they would see it differently. In the company of their Friend and Lord, they experienced a way of life they had not known before. They learned that they could share in Jesus' direct access to his infinitely loving *Abba* Father. They came to know themselves as recovering sinners, unconditionally accepted by their loving Creator. They received God's gifts of love, joy, and peace that Jesus alone could give them.

In this interactive communion with God's loving presence, they discovered spiritual resources to help them live more fully and creatively. They would not have considered being Jesus' disciples a bad deal.

Still today, Jesus offers himself to us as our risen Friend and Lord. He says, in his unique voice of love,

> *Follow me. I know you by name. I laid down my life for you and the whole world. I have done everything necessary to make freely available the kind of life for which your heart yearns. Come and live with me. I want to lead you, step by step, into an entirely different way of being. As you learn to follow me, every morning, every hour, every moment of every day, you will come to know me as your closest Friend*

> *and Companion. Your deepest desire to live in*
> *intimate communion with God will be satisfied,*
> *as well as deepened. Will you be my disciple,*
> *so that I may lead you along the way into your*
> *heart's true home?*

Now, let me ask you about your own response to this gospel invitation to discipleship: Would you describe yourself as a disciple of Jesus Christ? If the word *disciple* sounds off-putting or carries unhelpful baggage for you, then you may want to replace it with another word, like *learner*, *student*, or *follower*. The word that Dallas preferred was *apprentice*.

Please notice I am not asking whether you are a believer, or baptized, or confirmed, or even a Christian. I am asking whether you want to live as a disciple of Jesus. Reflect on your life today and ask yourself the question: *Do I desire to follow Jesus more closely?*

The Gospel Way of Discipleship

In order to clarify our response to this gospel invitation, we must ask the question: What most faithfully represents the gospel way of discipleship?

There are three possible ways of responding to this question. While the first two ways have important places in our discipleship journey, the third option is the most critical in our following of Jesus.

The Way of Information

Some see discipleship as accumulating more and more information about Jesus. They would tell us that, if we want to follow Jesus, we need to get to know as much as we can about him. We must find out about what he said and what he did. We must read about the way he died and rose from the dead.

Sometimes those who place information at the heart of discipleship may encourage us to supplement biblical knowledge with research into the first-century culture in which Jesus lived. We need, we are told, to get to know about the historical Jesus.

While learning about Jesus in this informative way is certainly important, there is more to following Jesus than acquiring facts about him. As followers of Jesus, we are always in a learning relationship with him, but not in the academic sense of studying in a lecture hall. Being a disciple is more than acquiring biblical and historical information.

The reason for this is obvious. Information, by itself, seldom transforms character. Being inwardly changed into God's compassionate image bearers involves much more than attending Bible studies. While Jesus' good news comes to us with clear content to it, inner transformation requires something more. After all, we can accumulate lots of knowledge about Jesus and yet remain totally un-Christlike in our character and behavior.

Here is one sad example. The divinity department of a certain South African university included some of the best lecturers in Old and New Testament studies, systematic theology, church history, pastoral ministry, and biblical languages. These men and women were experts in their fields of Christian academic study, effective in their communication of their subjects, and widely published in biblical and theological journals. But they could not get along with each other. The department was known for its conflict, the professors' inability to function together, and its leadership power struggles. Eventually, because of its ongoing relational dysfunction, it was closed by the vice chancellor and university board. As one of the professors said to me afterward, "We gave God a bad name."

We do well, however, not to throw stones at this department. All of us fail to be the compassionate Christ followers we know God calls us to be.

My own failures in basic ways of loving come quickly to mind.

Last year Debbie had a knee operation and then for ten days was confined to bed. It was my responsibility to care for her in her convalescence. Her requests were constant. "Please switch on the light." "I need a glass of water." "Turn on the fan." "Help me to the bathroom." By the third day, I needed all the resources of the Trinity to stay lovingly responsive.

Somehow it was easier for me to write about God's challenge to be loving than to joyfully respond to the needs of the one I love most. Even though I know quite a lot about Jesus, I failed dismally to reflect God's compassion in my closest relationship.

The Way of Inspiration

There is a great market for inspiring spiritual experiences today that promise quick and easy solutions for complex human struggles. This relentless lusting after inspirational "highs" usually leads toward the deadly pitfalls of consumer religion. This craving quickly turns you and me into religious consumers who go shopping on a weekly basis to find where we can get our next inspirational fix.

Again, I must be careful with my words. Being inspired by a moving worship moment, or a passionate proclamation of the good news, or an artist's beautiful expression of our faith, can be a source of tremendous encouragement. I have little doubt that Jesus inspired his first followers with his words and deeds. Likewise, we have also had inspirational moments that have reenergized, revitalized, and renewed us in our Christ following. These moments bring color, lightness, and vitality to our discipleship. Looking back on our spiritual history and identifying these lamplight experiences of the Spirit's presence and activity has a way of brightening our walk with God. I would not be writing these words without such inspiring moments illuminating my faith autobiography.

Inspiration alone, however, seldom transforms the destructive habits of our heart and mind.

Here is an imaginary scenario:

Let us say Tom is a regular churchgoer who has battled for years with a raging temper. Repeatedly, he explodes with outbursts of angry words toward those closest to him, leaving a trail of hurt and heartache. He hears that his church will be inviting "a powerful speaker with an inspirational and life-changing message" to come preach. At the service Tom is moved by the passionate words spoken about Christ's ability to transform the human heart. After the service, the guest preacher gives an invitation for anyone who would like to experience a changed life to come forward for prayer. Tom goes forward, hands are laid on him, and prayers are offered for him to receive the transforming power of God's Spirit.

While this moment could be a key advance in Tom's discipleship journey, it is unlikely that his explosive temper will be transformed in these few brief minutes. Indeed, if he is not helped to see what the gospel way of discipleship is, he may become disillusioned and feel despair when his anger gets the better of him again. He may conclude that all this talk about Christ transforming us is an illusion, or that God changes others but not him, or that God does not hear his prayers.

These conclusions, and others like them, cause many to look elsewhere in their spiritual search. This happens especially when we ignore the third option.

The Way of Interaction

Faithful gospel discipleship, I suggest, is to interact with Jesus Christ. This is what it meant for his first followers.

Go back to that beginning moment in his public ministry when Jesus announced the availability of another kind of life. Soon afterward he called Simon and Andrew to follow him.

Jesus wanted them to be with him and to enter a relationship in which they would come to know him for themselves.

They left their nets and followed him. Although they did not know where he was leading them, they trusted him and walked with him. While they acquired more information about him, and were inspired by his example and his words, interacting with him was the way they came to know him.

It was this interaction with Jesus that transformed those earliest disciples. The New Testament makes it clear that it was not an overnight transformation. It happened gradually as they spent time with Jesus, learned from him, and interacted with him. They came to know themselves as God's dearly beloved children. They experienced a new sense of belonging with each other. Their personalities were gradually renovated so that they became better images of God. They responded to others with a new seeing, a new listening, a new heart. They lived with a strong sense of God's power over evil, within and around them. They overcame their fear of those who could destroy their bodies. They entered another kind of life in which they became more and more like the one they followed.

At this point, you may be thinking, *I can see what following Jesus meant for those disciples then. When Jesus came to them in the flesh, they could physically interact with him. Little wonder they were transformed by their interaction with him. But what does it mean for us to interact with Jesus today? We cannot listen to him, question him, or touch him, like they did.*

This is a critical inquiry that we must explore as thought-fully as we can. Thankfully, as we seek to learn ways of inter-acting with Christ today, both Ignatius and Dallas come alongside us as trustworthy guides.

To Know, to Love, and to Follow

After catching a glimpse of the life God gives when he lay and read those two books on his sickbed in Loyola and follow-ing his time of honest confession and deepening repentance in Montserrat, Ignatius made his way to the small town of Manresa, where he stayed for almost eleven months. Here he wrestled deeply with what it means to be a faithful disciple of Jesus.

After an initial time of tranquility and consolation, he entered a time of extreme desolation. As he reflected upon these inner contrasting movements between consolation and desolation, he began making notes and putting together *Spiritual Exercises*.

Significantly, the Second Week has been described by some Ignatian scholars as a "school of discipleship."[1] As we trace the transition from the First to the Second Week, we can see why.

Recall what we said earlier about the First Week (page 64). There the focus is on knowing ourselves as beloved sinners. In the blazing light of God's never-giving-up and forgiving love, we asked God to show us the extent of our personal and social disorder.

Remember, too, how Ignatius invited us to look at the

face of the crucified Jesus and to receive his loving gaze of grace and mercy as we shared the mess and muck of our lives. He wanted us to know that our past failures in living and loving can never stop God reaching out to us. While this assurance of God's enduring love grows within us, we want to deepen our discipleship relationship with the Lord. As William Barry points out, "We are ready to allow the desire to know, love, and follow Christ to rise in our hearts."[2]

Hence, in the Second Week, we move from praying over the disorder in our world and in our lives toward praying over the life of Jesus Christ. During this phase of the *Spiritual Exercises*, Ignatius invites us to "ask for the grace to *know* Jesus intimately, to love him more intensely, and so to follow him more closely."[3]

The word *know* is an important biblical word. There are two ways of knowing that, while related, should be distinguished from each other.

First, we can know *about* someone. This is what I referred to earlier as "the way of information." This is not what Ignatius had in mind when, in the *Spiritual Exercises*, he encouraged us to ask for the grace to know Jesus intimately. We get to know someone in this way through "the way of interaction."

There are two important Greek words for "to know" in the Bible: *ginosko* and *oida*. The first signifies an objective knowledge of someone or something, while *oida* tends to mean a personal perception or appropriation of knowledge. Dallas Willard points out that philosophers similarly distinguish between "knowledge by *description*" and "knowledge by *acquaintance*." "Only the latter," he writes, "is the interactive relationship, the 'reality hook,' that gives us a grasp of the person or the thing 'itself.'"[4] When Ignatius used the word *know*, this second way of knowing was intended. To know Christ, in the biblical way, is not so much about getting more information about him; rather, it is about interacting with him in the here and now.

An essential part of this interaction is asking Jesus to reveal himself to us so that we may truly come to know him. We want to get to know Jesus' heart and mind, his attitudes and practices, his values and principles, his dreams and hopes, and most especially the nature of his intimate relationship with the one he called Abba.

Ignatius is confident that as we get to know Jesus in this intimate way, we will fall in love with him and desire to follow him more faithfully. This is the faithful gospel way of discipleship.

But how do we interact with the invisible Jesus *today*, so that we may get to know him like this? With thanks to Ignatius and Dallas, here are three inseparables from this journey.

Sharing in Intimate Conversation with Jesus

When I did the *Spiritual Exercises*, I was introduced to a word that I had not come across before. It was *colloquy*, which Ignatius puts at the end of each prayer exercise. He suggests that this is to be an intimate conversation, "as one friend speaks to another."[5]

Such conversation always goes two ways. It involves us both sharing ourselves honestly with the Lord and listening while he speaks to us. As we engage in colloquy, we reveal ourselves to Jesus and he reveals himself to us. This mutual self-revelation lies at the heart of our interactive relationship with the living Christ.[6]

We should not be surprised by this emphasis on mutual self-revelation. Think of any friendship in your life. How does this friendship deepen? Whenever you get together, both of you take turns talking and listening. You share how you are feeling and what you are doing, and you do your best to be attentive to what your friend shares as well. Both parts of the conversation—sharing and listening—are important if you are going to get to know each other.

What makes for good friendship with another human being holds true for our relationship with the living Christ as well. It deepens as we share with him what is going on in our lives right now and as we seek to be attentive to how he reveals himself to us.

The most important thing I have learned in sharing myself with the Lord is to be totally honest and transparent. This means sharing what I truly think and feel rather than what I believe I should say. This could involve sharing my doubts and disappointments, my anger and resentment, my loneliness and sadness, as well as my joy and gratitude. James Martin, SJ, well-known writer on Ignatian spirituality, sums it up for me when he writes, "Be honest with God about everything."[7]

When I talk with others about the importance of being honest with the Lord, some ask whether this is necessary. "Surely," they object, "he knows what we are going to say anyway."

My response to this is always the same. The purpose of being transparent with Christ is *not* to give him information. The purpose is to get to know him more intimately.

Some time ago, just before my daughter got married, she faced a lengthy operation on her jaw. On the Sunday before the surgery, Joni came to me and said, "I am scared about the operation." In that moment she was not telling me anything I did not know. She was sharing herself with me, opening her heart to me, and giving me greater access into her life. As a result, through being honest with me, she also got to know more deeply how I felt toward her. Her vulnerable sharing of herself gave me access to show her the depths of my care and concern. If she had not been open with me about her fear, this would not have happened as it did.

It is the same in our relationship with Jesus. When we tell him about our lives, it is not for the sake of information. Rather, we want to give him access to our lives. As we share ourselves honestly with him, we allow his grace and strength to enter our lives more deeply. We give him access to reveal his loving and strengthening presence in a more real way.

This is the reason why whenever we spend time alone with Jesus, Ignatius wants us to share aloud our thoughts and feelings with him. Through this kind of intimate interaction, our relationship moves in the direction of an ever-deepening closeness. We come to know the Lord more intimately, and in so doing, love him more intensely and follow him more faithfully.

Additionally, as in any good friendship, we need to listen to the Lord. This part of the conversation takes a bit longer to develop. We may find listening to someone we can see quite difficult; how much more so with someone we cannot see?

We have many questions. What does it mean to say that Jesus speaks to us? How do we know when it is Jesus speaking to us? How do we know that we are not just talking to ourselves?

Since we are usually unsure about how to answer these questions, our prayer often becomes a one-way conversation. This is not good for any friendship.

All these questions have been part of my own prayer journey. I have been gradually learning, whenever I share myself with the Lord, to also give him some space to respond. In my one-on-one time with the Lord, there are moments when I am silent. During these moments, as I think about what I have read in Scripture, or become part of a Gospel story, or reflect on my conversation with Christ, or ponder what's happening in my life, I pay attention to my thoughts and feelings. As I become attentive in this way, I am always wondering what the Lord may be sharing with me. (In chapter 6 I give attention to how we may discern Christ's presence and activity in these thoughts and feelings.)

SEEKING EXERCISE

Perhaps you can take a break from reading about colloquy in order to give yourself a few moments to share together with Jesus in intimate conversation where you are. Picture yourself sitting with Jesus. Share with the Lord whatever you are feeling and thinking right now about your relationship together. You may be feeling grateful, disappointed, content, angry, forsaken, serene, or yearning. Whatever your feelings may be, share them aloud with the Lord, as honestly as you can.

Afterward, be quiet for a few moments and be attentive to your own thoughts and feelings. How do you sense the Lord responding to you?

Keeping Jesus before Our Mind

In 1993, as I was driving Dallas Willard to the airport to catch his flight home, I said to him, "Dallas, as I seek to be a follower of Christ here in South Africa, I wonder if you have a word for me."

He was quiet for a few minutes while I kept my eyes on the road. Eventually he spoke. He simply said, "Trevor, guard your mind. The thoughts, images, and pictures in your mind matter. They shape your life."

Then, paraphrasing one of his favorite verses from the

Psalms, he added, "Make sure you keep the Lord before you always" (Psalm 16:8).

We drove the rest of the way to the airport mostly in silence. I turned his words over and over in my mind. I knew that learning to be conscious of the Lord through the day would be an essential ingredient of my discipleship journey from that moment onward.

We get to know Jesus Christ intimately, and to interact with him, primarily through the images, pictures, and thoughts in our mind. The Greek word for repentance, *metanoia*, makes this clear. It means "changing our mind," or as Dallas paraphrased the word, "thinking about our thinking."[8] Whereas prior to turning toward Christ we lived our lives without reference to Christ, we now have the desire to let him be the center of our attention and living.

For me—as Dallas had suggested on that drive to the airport—this would mean regularly turning my mind in a Christward direction. Learning how to keep the Lord before me in this way has become a daily practice. Without it, I realized, I would have little conscious interaction with Christ in the hurly-burly of everyday life.

How can we go about doing this? To begin with, we need to realize that we have some freedom as to where we choose to focus our minds. This choice affects our emotional landscape, our mental atmosphere, our reactions to current events, our responses to those around us, and most importantly, how we live.

The repeated choice of keeping the Lord before us in our

minds is not easy. Most of us develop mental habits that cause our thoughts to wander everywhere except toward Christ. Usually we get easily drawn toward whatever is worrying us or causing us to be fearful.

These thoughts then create anxious scenarios that gobble up the space in our minds. Thankfully, when we become more aware of these negative thought patterns, little spaces open in our minds to make other choices. This resetting of the direction of our thoughts requires both effort and practice.

We practice keeping Christ before us by frequently reminding ourselves of the closeness of his risen presence. Whether catching up on Facebook, sitting in the boardroom, in between appointments, typing emails, or working in the garden, we acknowledge God-with-us wherever we are. These repeated affirmations may take the shape of a short prayer inwardly whispered, or remembering a Bible verse, or a conscious in-breathing of the Spirit. Many find the thoughtful repetition of the name of Jesus to be helpful in re-establishing themselves more consciously in Christ's presence.

By keeping ourselves aware of God's nearness, we are not trying to artificially manufacture any spiritual experience. We are simply turning our minds toward Christ, whose presence fills all things and who is closer to us than we can ever dare to imagine.

During the national lockdown in South Africa for COVID-19, we were told to wash our hands with soap repeatedly throughout the day. This moment became sacramental for me. Every time I washed my hands, I would remember my baptism. I would remind myself that I am God's beloved, loved with a love that knows me by name and will not let me go. Gently, I would turn my anxious mind again in the direction of the Lord and open myself to his Spirit. Washing hands like this twenty to thirty times each day helped me to live with a deeper sense of Christ before me each day.

When we experiment in this regard, we will quickly discover the life-transforming benefits of setting our mind on Christ. These will be different for each one of us. For some it will be a more definite sense of the divine presence in the ordinariness of their daily lives. They discover that Christ becomes an ever-present comfort in the stresses and strains of everyday life. Others become more responsive and attentive to people around them. They begin seeing those around them as God's unique and precious image bearers. Then there will be those who, as they keep Christ before them, engage their mundane tasks with a renewed motivation to honor God in all they do. They have a greater understanding of what displeases God in their daily endeavours.

SEEKING EXERCISE

During the next twenty-four hours, experiment with one of these ways of keeping Christ before your mind. Acknowledge his presence with you through the day by recalling a biblical verse, or repeating the name of Jesus, or touching a small cross in your pocket. Purposely intend to journey through this coming day with a deeper consciousness of his presence with and in you. You may want to make a few notes afterward of how this experience was for you.

Keeping Company with Jesus in the Gospels

One of the special gifts that Dallas gave me was the space to ask him questions. The first time I asked whether I could raise some questions with him, he responded with his typical generosity. We set one whole evening aside and sat together in our living room. I had with me a yellow pad to write down his responses to my long list of prepared questions. These ranged from theological issues that had come up for me, ethical dilemmas around some of the political issues facing us in South Africa at that dark time in our history, and the more practical concerns of what it meant to follow Jesus in the nitty-gritty of daily life.

Looking back on that evening now, I realize that my opening question was designed to impress him a bit. I asked him if he would provide me with a reading list of the most formative books that he had read. I recall how the conversation unfolded.

"I suggest you read Matthew, Mark, Luke, and John" was his reply.

Somewhat disappointed by this response, I told him, "Okay, I have got that down. Are there any other books you recommend that I read?"

This time he was more emphatic in his response. "My suggestion is that you take the next twenty years or so to read and meditate on these four Gospels. Read them repeatedly, immerse yourself in the words and deeds of Jesus, and commit to memory as much as you are able."

Now, I knew that Dallas took the whole of Scripture with the utmost seriousness. Once Jane Willard showed me one of his Bibles. I did not see one page unmarked. There were notes in the margin, underlined verses, additional cross-references that he had made on every page. So his recommendation that I repeatedly read the Gospels expressed his conviction that, if I wanted to interact with Jesus as his disciple, I must keep company with him in the Gospels.

I suspect that Ignatius would strongly agree with Dallas. Almost all the biblical material for the *Spiritual Exercises* is taken from the Gospels.

While reliably grounded in history, the Gospels are imaginative literature meant to draw us into a relationship with Jesus that is ongoing. In the Second Week Ignatius invites us to keep company with Jesus at his birth in Bethlehem, during his hidden life in Nazareth, at his baptism in the Jordan, in his wilderness temptations, when he called his disciples, throughout his public life and ministry, right up to his entry into Jerusalem on that first Palm Sunday. All the time, as we live imaginatively with Jesus throughout these Gospel scenes, we ask the Lord for the grace to come to know him more intimately, to love him more intensely, and to follow him more closely. Countless women and men can testify that Jesus has revealed himself to them as they prayed through these Gospel stories of Jesus.

This practice of keeping company with Jesus in the Gospels is not an encounter with a dead historical figure. The one with whom we interact is the one who lives beyond crucifixion, someone who is present with us in the here and now. The Jesus of history and the Christ of faith is the same person. As we read and pray through the Gospels with an open heart and open mind, we can expect the one with whom we interact to step out of the pages and reveal himself to us as an ever-present reality.

The Gospels offer us far more than information and inspiration. When read with expectant trust and faith, they make interaction with the living Jesus a living reality.

Imaginative Prayer

One of Ignatius's favorite ways of praying was to step into a Gospel story imaginatively. Although Ignatius was not the first to pray in this way, he gives imaginative prayer an important place in the *Spiritual Exercises*.

From the Second Week onward, those engaged in the Exercise journey enter the different Gospel scenes as though they are part of it. They learn how to live in the story, to be with the different characters involved, and to interact with Jesus as they are drawn to do so. Afterward, they reflect on their prayer experience and make notes on how it was for them.

On my last eight-day retreat, I was directed by a Jesuit

familiar with this way of prayer. At nine o'clock each morning, I would meet him in his little office to share how my time in the past day of prayer had gone. He would then suggest a Scripture passage with which I could pray during the coming day.

One morning I came into the session, my head full of insights about the Gospel passage in John 21 he had given me the previous day. Besides praying with this encounter between Jesus and Peter, I had found a Bible commentary in the library and made some notes in my journal of some fresh discoveries about this passage. I wanted to share these insights with my veteran retreat guide.

As we took our seats, he asked me how my prayer had gone the day before. I told him about going to the library and how I had come across these helpful insights into the passages that he given me. I started reading my notes to him.

Instead of sharing my excitement about my new learnings, he looked decidedly unimpressed. Halfway through what I was sharing, he interrupted me. With a twinkle in his eyes, he leaned over and said, "Trevor, insight is the consolation prize. The first prize is encounter with Jesus."

Again, I realized how easily I turn my times of prayer into a head trip, where I collect more insights about Jesus rather than personally interacting with him.

With a smile, my retreat guide suggested that I return to the Gospel encounter between Jesus and Peter, dwell within it imaginatively, and let Jesus encounter me in whatever way he chose to do so.

For the rest of that day, I lived in this Gospel story. The scene came alive for me as I looked and listened with my inner eyes and ears. I found myself drawn into conversation with Jesus about where I found myself in my life, and I sensed his presence with me, inviting me to stay close to him and follow him into the unknown future.

The following morning, I shared with my companion how I had interacted with Jesus in my time of imaginative prayer. Our conversation had a completely different quality of aliveness and energy compared to the day before, when I had read aloud my carefully collected list of intellectual insights.

Practical Steps

Because imaginative prayer can easily be misunderstood, let me briefly explain how it may look in practice. We begin our time of prayer by sharing with Jesus our desire to know him more intimately, love him more intensely, and follow him more closely. We do not want to gather more information about the Gospel reading, however useful that may be, but rather we want to know Jesus. We then read the Gospel story a few times until we have a clear sense of its details. When we are at home in it, we imagine that it is happening now. We place ourselves in the story, maybe as one of the characters or as ourselves. We participate in whatever happens in the Gospel story, observing what is happening with all our senses. Most crucially of all, we interact with Jesus, sharing with him whatever thoughts and feelings rise in our heart and mind, asking him to let us see beyond his words and actions to know his heart and mind and listening to how he responds to us.

The crucial step we take is the step of faith that the Jesus in the Gospel story is the living Lord present with us in the here and now. He is the same yesterday, today, and forever (Hebrews 13:8). Nor does he have a bad memory; he remembers every bit of his own experience on earth.

As we pray a Gospel story imaginatively, we trust that the risen Christ will reveal whatever he wants to share with us. It is not so much going back in history and trying to recreate a scene that happened a long time ago. Rather, it is trusting that he will come to us, in our circumstances and world, with our struggles and weaknesses, with a similar compassion or concern or challenge with which he came to the person in the Gospel story that we have just read. As we pour out our heart to him and welcome him into our life, he reveals his heart toward us. We encounter and interact with the living Christ.

In imaginative prayer, we place our imagination at the service of our faith. Through this God-given faculty, we can interact with Christ and he can connect with us. Of course, we know that the image is not the reality. Exercising our imagination in this way simply deepens our participation in the reality that it seeks to describe. Nor do we assume that everything that happens in our imagination comes from the Lord. Much can be put down to our own projections and wishes. But I am learning to pay careful attention to those surprises that come to me in my times of imaginative prayer, especially those that reveal Jesus more intimately to me and cause me to love him more intensely and follow him more closely.

Often sharing our experience of imaginative prayer with a small group or with a spiritual director will help us get a sense of how the Spirit of the risen Christ has been with us in our praying.

SEEKING EXERCISE

Take a few moments to experiment with imaginative prayer. Choose your favorite Gospel story. Read through it a few times to reacquaint yourself with the details. Put the Bible down and ask God for the grace to come to know, love, and follow Christ more deeply. Step into the scene as a participant rather than as a spectator. See the persons involved, hear the words spoken, watch the actions performed. Pay attention to where you find yourself in the story. What do you see? What do you hear? How do you feel? What goes through your mind? Above all, interact with Christ as he meets you in this story, share whatever is on your heart with him, and listen to what he may be saying to you. Afterward make a few notes of how it went for you.

Life's Greatest Opportunity

I hope you have caught a glimpse of the gospel way of discipleship. To be a disciple of Jesus is to be with him and interact with him. This interaction with Jesus today happens as we get to know him, set our mind on him, and keep company with him in the Gospels.

When this interaction with Jesus is genuine, it changes us inwardly and outwardly. We catch glimpses of Jesus' intimacy with *Abba* Father and begin to share in it ourselves. We feel drawn into community with others, as those around him in the Gospels were. God's compassionate family likeness starts rubbing off on us a little bit more. There is a greater strength within us to do what is right and refuse what is evil. We know that nothing, not even death, can separate us from God's love in Christ our Lord (Romans 8:38-39).

In summary, we experience another kind of life, the life that God gives. Can you see why discipleship has been called "life's greatest opportunity"?[9]

We respond to the call of Jesus to be his disciple, not because he meets all our needs, or fixes all our problems, or fills us with nice feelings. In fact, despite following Jesus, I sometimes find life extremely difficult and perplexing.

We follow Jesus because he shows us how to seek and find the *zoe* life that his *Abba* Father gives.

You may disagree with this rather dogmatic-sounding claim about Jesus. "Surely," I can hear you saying, "there are numerous other ways to live which are equally meaningful."

When I am challenged like this, a story drawn from the life of Dallas comes to mind. A philosophy doctoral student once asked him, "Professor, why do you, an intelligent, thoughtful, and well-educated man, follow Jesus?"

With characteristic respect and courtesy, he responded with a question of his own. "Tell me," he asked the inquiring student, "whom else do you have in mind?"[10]

He was not being flippant. He was saying, "I believe Jesus was the greatest, the smartest, and best person who has ever lived on this earth. If you can show me someone better, I will gladly follow him."

SEEKING EXERCISE

I close this chapter by urging you to respond personally to Jesus' invitation to be his disciple. Here is one way you can do this: Read your Beloved Charter, if you have put one together (page 68). Remind yourself that as God's dearly beloved, you have been sought by a great and passionate Love from your earliest beginnings. Allow the bloody fact of the Calvary execution to emphasize in your heart and mind the heart-wrenching goodness of God and the infinite largeness of God's scandalous mercy and forgiveness. Imagine the living and risen Christ, still with his wounds of crucified love, standing before you, as he stood before the earliest disciples, calling you by name to follow him into the life that God gives.

If you want, respond by saying this prayer:

Dear Lord Jesus Christ, your unconditional love and gracious call have burned into my heart. Now, in loving response for all that you have done, I entrust myself as completely as I can to you as my Savior, Teacher, Lord, and Friend. Please give me a heartfelt and intimate knowledge of who you are, that I may come to love you more intensely and follow you more closely. Fill me with the enabling power of your Spirit and show me how to live my life as you would if you were in my place. I ask for these things with all the love and longing of my heart, that I may live in your eternal Kingdom, now and forever.

CHAPTER 6

DYING TO LIVE

Jesus didn't die on the cross so that we don't have to.
He died on the cross so that we may join him there.

DALLAS WILLARD

OVER THE YEARS, my understanding of what it means to follow Jesus has been profoundly shaped by single sentences either in books that I have read or have been spoken to me. These are those unforgettable words that scorch their way into our memory banks with lasting impact. When reading *The Cost of Discipleship* in my early twenties, this was my experience when I came across that startling line, "When Christ calls a man, he bids him come and die."[1]

When I first read those words, I had little idea of their meaning for my own life. I knew what they had meant for Bonhoeffer. He was executed by the Nazis for his active resistance efforts in the name of the gospel. But what did they mean within the ordinary relationships of everyday life? While I intuitively recognized that these words were critical for our life of discipleship, their practical relevance remained unclear for me for some years. The sentence, however, kept reverberating in my heart and mind.

Gradually, I began to realize that these words reveal the heartbeat of gospel discipleship: *If we truly want to know the life God gives us at its best, its deepest, its most flourishing, we need to learn to die daily.* While this may not involve literal martyrdom, it will mean dying to all those aspects of our lives that prevents us from becoming the loving person God wants us to be. Life through death describes the pattern of authentic Christ following.

To listen more attentively to this heartbeat as we seek to follow Jesus, let us step into a Gospel story.

We Want to See Jesus

In John 12, we read how some Greeks approached Jesus' disciple Philip and said they wanted to see Jesus. They had heard about him; now they desired to see him.

We have already seen in the previous chapter how crucial this distinction is. The Greeks wanted to know Jesus personally rather than to only know *about* him in a secondhand way.

We can accumulate lots of knowledge about Jesus by attending Sunday school classes, hearing sermons, listening to podcasts, and reading books. We must, however, encounter Jesus to know him firsthand. This lifelong seeking adventure begins when, like these Greek seekers, we express our desire to see and know Jesus for ourselves. We do this, as we saw in the previous chapter, by simply asking him to reveal his heart to us so that we come to know him more intimately, love him more deeply, and follow him more closely.

Now back to the Gospel story. Philip went to Andrew, then they both went together to Jesus with this request. Intriguingly, Jesus did not respond, "That's great! Bring them to me right now, and they can see me for themselves." His answer was more indirect. He offered them an image of a single seed dying in order to bring forth abundant fruit.

Recall Jesus' words: "Very truly, I tell you, unless a grain of wheat falls into the earth and dies, it remains a single grain; but if it dies, it bears much fruit" (John 12:24). Hidden in these words is the invitation to hear the heartbeat of gospel discipleship: We experience the fullness of life that God offers through dying.

Like all Gospel images, there are several layers of meaning to this one. Let us begin to dig, keeping one foot in this Gospel encounter and the other in our own seeking lives.

The Cross of Jesus

When Jesus spoke about a seed being planted in the ground and then dying, he was referring primarily to his own death. Just like a seed that falls into the ground and dies, so he would go to the cross and die. There he would pour his life out in self-giving love, absorb the powers of evil and darkness, and die at the hands of religious leaders working in tandem with those in political power.

His death on the cross would seem to be a terrible failure, a devastating defeat, a tragic ending. Who could ever believe in a crucified Messiah? By conventional definition, a dead Messiah was a failed Messiah. With this striking image, however, Jesus turned upside down the disciples' understanding of what it meant for him to be the Messiah. Rather than be a violent political Messiah, he would be God's suffering Servant-King.

Notice that the seed in the image does not end in death. If the seed died, Jesus made clear, it would bring new life and bear much fruit. While outwardly his death would look like a failure, it was a glorious victory of the divine Love over the dark powers of evil, sin, and death.

As New Testament scholar Tom Wright explains in his reflection on this seed image, Jesus' death would be "the triumph of God's self-giving love, the love that looks death itself in the face and defeats it by meeting it voluntarily, on behalf not just of Israel but of the whole world, the world represented by these 'Greeks.'"[2] The way of this Messiah would be totally different from the violent ways of all other wannabe messiahs. The power of love, as revealed in the cross of Jesus, would triumph over the love of power.

One of the first steps in my training toward becoming a Methodist minister was to study the different atonement theories. I can still remember how inadequate I felt as I sought to plumb the unfathomable depths of the crucifixion and what it means for us. Tragically, there have been many painful controversies within the Christian church as to which atonement theory is the "right" one. After many years of study, I have come to see that the Cross has many different sides, each of which has rich meanings. We always need to hold these different meanings together.

The various meanings of the "many-sided Cross" invite much thought and reflection. The Cross reveals the extent to which God goes to demonstrate divine love. Nothing can stop God loving us in Christ. Moreover, not only does the crucified God understand our pain, but God shares it. In some mysterious way, we witness Jesus on the cross taking our place and dying instead of us. The image of the sacrificial Lamb was a powerful metaphor for the first Jewish believers. On the cross we also see the victory of God over all the "principalities and powers" that spoil and sabotage human life. All these meanings (and there are others) stretch our small minds as we look at the crucified Christ who stands at the center of history.

Thankfully, we don't need to understand every atonement theory to know the transforming power of the Cross. Its undeniable power to transform us is a simple fact, confirmed by human experience.

A Catholic archbishop described how three mischievous teenage boys decided to play a trick on their local priest. While he was hearing confessions one day, they took turns going into the confessional and admitting to doing all sorts of fantastic things that they had made up.

A young boy volunteered to be the first one. However, the priest was not to be fooled and said to him, "I want you to make this penance for what you have done. Go to the front of the church, to the cross on which Jesus hangs, look Jesus in the face, and say three times, 'All this you did for me, and I don't give a damn.'"

The teenager did it once, twice, and then, when he began repeating the sentence a third time, broke down in tears, and his words simply became, "You did this for me." He left the church facing a new direction.

When the archbishop finished the story, he said, "The reason I know this is that I was that young man."[3]

Perhaps you have known the power of the Cross in this real, rough, and robust way. This is what happened for me at the beginning of my faith journey. As a teenager, with no formal church background and no theological learning, I was ambushed by the love of God revealed through the crucified Jesus. Somehow through the Cross I had the sense of God saying to me, "This is what I will go through for you. This is how much you mean to me. Nothing can stop me from loving you."

The sheer fact of the Cross is, as Dallas would say, something we must keep before us all the time. As he wrote, "The divine conspiracy of which I am a part stands over history in the form of a cross."[4]

Our Cross

When Jesus used the image of a seed dying and then creating new life, he was also describing the way *we* must go. This was his challenge to the Greeks. If they really wanted to know him personally, to see him for themselves, then like a seed they would also have to fall into the ground and die.

Throughout the Gospels, we come across Jesus' insistence that those who follow him must learn how to die. Think of what he once said: "If any want to become my followers, let them deny themselves and take up their cross daily and follow me. For those who want to save their life will lose it, and those who lose their life for my sake will save it" (Luke 9:23-24).

Can you see the two crosses in the New Testament—the unique cross of Jesus and the cross that belongs to us? Like a seed that falls to the ground and dies, we die so we can bear much fruit. This is Jesus' cross-shaped life, in which we are invited to share. We cannot bypass the cross. There are no shortcuts on the discipleship pathway.

If we want to find the fullness of life that Jesus spoke about, we must learn how to die. *Zoe* life comes through dying. At the heart of discipleship there is a death to self that we need to embrace. This invitation certainly does not sound very inviting when we first hear it.

Here, we must clarify that we are dealing with death *to* self, not death *of* self.[5] Jesus does not want us to get rid of ourselves. Nor does he want us to self-depreciate or think that we are worthless. We were not loved into existence by God so that our lives would count for nothing. We are called to be all who God wants us to be, to come alive to the wonder of our own beautiful uniqueness, to live the distinctiveness of our one life as completely as possible. If we are to become this fully alive person, however, we must die to those aspects of ourselves that keep us from growing in this direction.

It must also be clarified that, when Jesus taught like this, he was not laying a heavy burden on us. Always the master of reality, Jesus knew how life works. Seeds must die if they are to grow fruit.

Think of a mathematics teacher who tells her students, "Unless you master arithmetic, you cannot do algebra," or a language teacher who says, "Unless you learn the letters of the alphabet, you cannot begin to read." They are not making things difficult for their students. That's simply the way things work.[6]

Likewise, Jesus wanted his disciples to be clear about the heartbeat of discipleship. Unless they took up their cross daily and learned how to die, they would not experience the fruitful abundance of another kind of life.

Denying Ourselves

These important Gospel words about denying ourselves and taking up our cross daily prompt a few more clarifying thoughts.[7]

First, as we have seen, to deny ourselves does not mean that we must put ourselves down, or undervalue ourselves, or have a low self-image. Earlier we saw the importance of creating a Beloved Charter that helps us to see ourselves through God's loving gaze. We can celebrate our infinite worth as God's beloved sinners. Yet, while we recognize ourselves as God's image bearers, we must not put ourselves at the center of our lives. As Christ followers, this central place belongs to God alone. To deny ourselves means that, through our ongoing surrender to Christ, our lives slip over into a new divine center. No longer do we take center stage; now we want God to reign in our lives.

Next, denying ourselves involves taking up our cross. We sometimes trivialize this invitation by linking it with some irritating feature in our lives. It means far more than this. It is dying to our self-centeredness, selfishness, and self-interest. When we put God at the hub of our lives, we are exposed to the bright light of God's self-giving love in a new way. Touched by these rays, our eyes are opened to the hidden depths of our egocentricity. It gets uncovered in all its tricks of hiding and pretending, falsity and fear. We see more clearly how much our selfishness and dishonesty have hurt others, especially those closest to us. Learning to die to these self-centered patterns of our behavior is what our "dying" looks like.

Last, taking up our cross is something that we need to do each day. Putting Christ at the center of our lives introduces into our lives a new inner battle. There remains a deeply ingrained part of ourselves that still wants to call the shots, to be in control, to do things our way. The only way through this ongoing struggle into the freedom of another kind of life is our daily willingness to deny ourselves. We take up the cross, day after day after day.

Implementing this firm resolution, with the strength that our friendship with God gives us, creates the necessary climate for God's fruit to ripen within us.

The Fruit of Compassion

What is this divine fruit that grows in us as we learn how to die?

Here are my best thoughts around this critical question: The God whom we meet in the Bible is the God of compassion. This compassionate God loves us with a faithful love, came to be with us, and wants to be friends with us.

Bible scholars point out that the Hebrew words translated *compassion* and *womb* are the same word except for having different vowels. God's compassion is the same kind of other-centered, self-giving, and sacrificial love that a mother has for her child.

Mothers will go to great lengths for their children, often sacrificing themselves greatly for the sake of their well-being. Isaiah explores the imagery of God's motherly womb love beautifully:

> Can a woman forget her nursing child,
> or show no compassion for the child of her womb?
> Even though she may forget,
> yet I will not forget you.
>
> ISAIAH 49:15

We see God's compassion vividly demonstrated in both the teaching and the life of Jesus. Think of Jesus' description of the prodigal's father when he welcomed his young son home: "But while he was still a long way off, his father saw him and was filled with compassion" (Luke 15:20, NIV). Jesus' basic conviction was that the One whom he called "Abba" relates to us like the loving father in this parable. He was utterly convinced that compassion filled the entire being of God. Like the sun that keeps shining, so God's compassion radiates toward us constantly. It can do nothing else. Jesus's words in this parable reveal God to you and me as the Compassionate One who will never stop showing compassion to us.

We also witness God's compassion in the actions of Jesus. If there is one defining virtue in Jesus' life, it is this. Compassion characterized all his responses, especially toward the vulnerable. It was with compassion that Jesus touched the leper, fed the hungry, opened the eyes of the blind, and looked out upon the crowd who were like sheep without a shepherd (see Matthew 9:36, 20:34; Mark 1:41, 8:2). The Jesus we meet in the Gospels was walking, talking, living, breathing compassion.

The Greek phrase used by the New Testament writers, "to be moved with compassion," is only used with reference to Jesus and to his Abba Father. The relevant verb, *splagchnizomai*, speaks of the incredible depths of compassion in God's heart. As author and priest Henri Nouwen, known for his many helpful books on the spiritual life, movingly wrote, "When Jesus was moved to compassion, the source of all life trembled, the ground of all love burst open, and the abyss of God's immense, inexhaustible, and unfathomable tenderness revealed itself."[8]

For this reason, I believe that the chief fruit of the seed

that dies is compassion. Because God is the Compassionate One, we reflect the divine family likeness best when we show compassion. Little wonder that Jesus said to his followers, "Be compassionate just as your Father is compassionate" (Luke 6:36, CEB). This could also be why, when Jesus spoke of the fruit that grows when the seed dies, he joined this image with other discipleship themes of losing our lives to find them and giving our lives in sacrificial servanthood to others. All three ingredients, when held together, unite in the fruit of compassion. To become more Christlike is to become more compassionate.

Now we can see that the acid test of discipleship is not how much we pray, or how much we know about the Bible, or whether we exercise the gifts of the Spirit, or even how involved we are in the struggle for justice. All these things are vitally important and have a crucial place in our following Jesus. When it comes to gauging the genuineness of our discipleship, however, these factors are not the most important. The acid test of whether we are becoming mature as a Christ follower is learning to deny ourselves and to die to selfishness so that the fruit of divine compassion grows within us. When this happens, our heartbeat begins to pulse in harmony with God's compassionate heartbeat.

Being Compassionate toward Jesus

Strikingly, the most important grace that we seek when we enter the Third Week of the Spiritual Exercises is the gift of compassion. Ignatius believed this compassion was the fruit of an ever-deepening intimacy with the crucified Jesus, as we seek to stay close with him, right to the end of his life. While we imaginatively contemplate the events in the last week of Jesus' life, beginning with the Last Supper, Ignatius invites us to ask for the grace of entering "sorrow and shame as I stay with Jesus in his sufferings borne on our behalf and because of our sins."⁹ This compassion that "suffers with" is a grace, something that God gives us as we seek to be present with Jesus during his passion.

I hope you are catching a glimpse of the flow of the *Spiritual Exercises*. In the First Week, we asked for the grace to know more deeply that we were beloved sinners. During the Second Week, we sought to get to know Jesus more intimately, love him more intensely, and follow him more closely. Now, in the Third Week, we want to follow Jesus to the end and be with him in his suffering and death.

We express our desire to be with him with words like "Lord, I want to stay with you to the Cross. Show me what this time of loneliness and rejection was like for you. Reveal to me your compassionate heart that was willing to lay your life down for us all. Help me to be present with you in your anguish." Only Jesus himself can reveal what he went through during these desolate days. As we share "the fellowship of His suffering," as Paul put it, we find our way into compassion (Philippians 3:10, NASB).

Can you see that the focus here in the Exercises is not to concentrate on our own suffering but to be with Jesus in the suffering he went through (and continues to go through in those who suffer today)? We seek to come close to Jesus, and feel with him, in his time of anguish and loss.

Ignatius wants us not just to know *about* the Passion; he wants us to enter it with Jesus. But we cannot manufacture this depth of compassion by our own efforts alone. So, as we seek to be with Jesus in his passion, Ignatius encourages us to ask God to grow our capacity to be compassionately present with his Son. This growth gradually happens as we die to our self-interest and egocentricity, to be more present to the Crucified One.

Both from doing the Third Week and from leading others through it, I have seen just how powerfully transformative this way of praying is. Although we cannot change what happened to Jesus, we can seek to be with him as he shares his experience of suffering and death with us. Often this is not easy. We feel his pain and are unable to do anything about it. Yet, as we stay with Jesus in prayer, he reveals his compassion-filled heart to us.

This encounter changes us. We realize how difficult it is to really be *with* someone who is suffering, especially when they are facing something we cannot change. Often there is little we can do and very little we can say. But through our intimacy with Jesus on the cross, his compassion flows into us and through us to others. The fruit grows.

Fifteen years after Ignatius's time in Manresa, where he started to put together the *Spiritual Exercises*, he had what we might call today "a peak experience." He and two companions were traveling to Rome. They had just been ordained and were on their way to offer themselves to serve their church. Ignatius was struggling with questions about how best he could serve God. He still cherished the dream of going to Jerusalem and serving the people there.

Just outside Rome, they came across a small chapel at La Storta. Ignatius walked ahead and went into the chapel on his own. He expressed his longing to know God's guidance in a simple prayer request: "Please place me with your Son." What happened next is significant for our reflections.

As an answer to this prayer, Ignatius was given a vision in which two persons of the Trinity appeared to him—the Father and the risen Christ, carrying his cross. He heard the words "I will be favorable to you in Rome." Then, in the vision, the Father turned to Jesus and said, "I want you to take this man to serve us." And Jesus—the risen Christ carrying his cross—said to Ignatius, "We want you to serve us." This image affirmed for Ignatius that carrying the cross would always be central to his life of discipleship. *Zoe* life would come through dying.

From this moment onward, Ignatius's life, and the lives of his companions, became increasingly marked by the fruit of compassion, as they died to their own dreams and gave their lives away in mission and service.

Being Compassionate toward Others

The fruit of compassion that comes from our deepening intimacy with the crucified Jesus permeates all our relationships, especially with those in pain and anguish. Our hearts of stone become hearts of flesh. Fresh stirrings rise within us to care for those going through difficult times. Like Jesus, we also find ourselves moved by compassion at times. When we act on these inner promptings toward compassion, God brings blessing to others in life-giving ways that often astound us. More importantly, we begin to be a compassionate image bearer where it matters most—in our everyday relationships with those around us. We pass the acid test of genuine discipleship.

William Barry describes how these inner stirrings or movements toward compassion happen in the most ordinary situations.[10] Always, we must choose whether we respond or not.

I think of some recent personal examples.

- A thought suddenly came to me to contact a colleague who had gone through an operation, but it would mean taking the time to go to her home when I was facing some pressing work deadlines. *Do I take the time to visit, which will increase my work pressure, or do I keep to my schedule so I can meet my deadlines?*

- A member of the congregation where I ministered some years ago called and shared his struggle with depression. I felt a surge of concern. *Should I get involved, or do I suggest he see someone else?*

- Right now, as I'm writing this, Debbie is beginning to make supper. I want to help with the cooking, but I also want to finish this section on compassion!

Certainly, we cannot act on every compassionate prompting. Each one raises dilemmas that invite discernment. How do we balance being compassionate toward ourselves with being compassionate toward others? When do the needs of our neighbor take precedence over our own? Which inner promptings come from God's Spirit, and which arise from our selfish need to be needed? How do we best reflect God's family likeness in the human struggles taking place on our streets?

Learning to express God's compassion, as Jesus did, is seldom straightforward. It is a lifetime journey that requires reflection, discernment, and wisdom.

If we put God's compassion into practice, we will need all the grace God gives.

About three years ago, a friend was diagnosed with Lou Gehrig's disease, an incurable and degenerative nervous-system illness. I assured him that I would visit weekly. As his condition worsened, I found it more and more difficult to simply sit by his bed. He could hardly speak, he breathed with difficulty, and he would only look at me. I felt helpless as I sat there.

When I arrived at his home one day, I just couldn't go in. I sat in the car outside his gate and messaged Debbie, sharing my resistance.

She responded with both encouragement and a challenge. "Trevor, it's the most important thing you are doing right now. Just go inside and be there with him, as fully present and attentive as you can be."

The fruit of compassion, which we ask for in the Third Week, is essentially to be lovingly present to those around us, especially those who suffer. Here we find the essence of a genuine Christ-following life. Any spirituality that does not make us more compassionate can hardly be called Christian. This fruit expresses itself in loving deeds, but at its heart, it involves being with others in their need.

Without the help and resources of God's Spirit, we will not progress very far down this road. The gospel call to reflect divine compassion is seldom easy and often challenging. And like the seed that must fall into the ground before it can bear fruit, it requires dying daily if we want God's compassion to grow in us.

SEEKING EXERCISE

Here are a few questions to help you consider what may be blocking growth of the fruit of compassion in your life. Take a few moments to ask yourself: What makes compassion hard in my everyday family and work relationships? In what ways does the call to compassion cause inconvenience in my life? What keeps me from being compassionately present and attentive to those nearest to me?

As you reflect on these questions, share with God your struggles to live the compassionate life. Remember that Christ always draws the starting line right where we are.

Learning to Die Daily

Let me restate one more time the central idea of this chapter: *If we truly want to know the life God gives at its gospel best, its deepest, its most flourishing, we need to learn how to die.* The seed needs to fall into the ground and die before it can bear fruit. Sharing in the compassion of God means denying ourselves and taking up our cross each day. This is how we follow Jesus into another kind of life, with all its remarkable blessings of joy and peace and freedom.

When Dallas Willard was a student at Tennessee Temple, he came across a little booklet called *How to Die Daily*. It had a life-shaping effect on him and his wife, Jane. Early in their marriage, it led them both to submit their bodies to God as a living sacrifice. During his graduate studies, he faced a constant challenge to die to arrogance, vanity, and self-certainty.

When I introduced Dallas at meetings in South Africa, he would urge me to keep the introduction brief. I remember him once saying, half-jokingly, that we should introduce speakers at Christian conferences in terms of their current weaknesses. "But" he said, "I haven't had any takers yet for this idea."

It was, however, Dallas's marriage relationship that became his most important learning space. After the death of their twins, Dallas and Jane became closer than they had ever been before. In the sacrificial way they sought to be there for each other in their grief, they learned what it meant to die daily.

We catch glimpses of what this "dying to self" looked like for Dallas in a talk he gave about being attentive and loving well. Speaking from the wisdom gained in his own experience, he said,

> You have to discipline your egoism. If you want to listen to others, you have to realize that you're not the most important person in the room. Because listening means that you cease to think about how you're doing and how they're thinking about you, and you stop adjusting your façade with words and thinking about how you are going to get the next bright remark in when you get a chance and you really, generously open yourself to the other person and receive them in love for what they are and stop worrying about yourself.[11]

Can you hear the heartbeat of discipleship?

Everyday Learning Opportunities

Learning to die daily is not an abstract concept. Each day presents us with opportunities to fall into the ground like a seed that dies, to deny ourselves, and to take up our cross. We can begin to practice dying right now. Sometimes it is these practice runs in compassionate living that reveal the true condition of our hearts.

Catch a few glimpses of what these "practice runs" may look like for us: listening attentively to someone else's struggle even when we are going through a difficult time, or responding to an email from a troubled person when we are feeling overwhelmed ourselves, or going the extra mile to give practical assistance to a friend, or driving out of our way to give a lift to someone without transport, or offering to babysit for a young couple so they can have an evening out, or giving attention to a colleague's requests as we seek to do our own work. And the list of opportunities to give our lives away in compassionate love goes on and on.

It is in these unspectacular, seemingly trivial moments that we can learn to die daily so that the fruit of divine compassion may ripen within us. As we practice dying in the smaller things, not only do we train for when greater sacrifices in loving will be demanded but we also live out God's compassion for those around us.

Let me describe a time when I was on the receiving end of such a compassionate action.

After my last eight-day retreat ended, I needed to get to the airport to catch my plane, which was leaving the Boston airport at 6:00 a.m. When I asked the retreat giver for the phone number of the local Uber service, he offered to take me himself. Because I knew that he had a full day ahead of him seeing other retreatants, this offer touched me deeply. Even more so when he greeted me with a smile at the unearthly hour of 3:30 a.m. in the parking lot, with no hint that I was putting him out. Through this simple act of receiving a lift, which no one else witnessed, my life was touched by God's compassion.

To be sure, there will be many times when we fail to respond to inner stirrings of compassion. We don't need to beat ourselves up. As disciples of Jesus, we remain lifelong learners. We have changed the direction of our lives. We are now citizens of a new Kingdom, where the last are first, the weak are strong, and those who lead are servants. We want to learn all we can about this unfamiliar Kingdom and how we participate in it.

The new language of this Kingdom—the language of a self-giving and sacrificial compassion—will take a lifetime to learn. Whenever we realize that we have failed to speak this language fluently, we simply turn to the Compassionate One and say, "Lord, I have made a mess again. I need your help. May your compassion cover my mistakes and flow through me more freely."

SEEKING EXERCISE

Right now, I wonder where you may need to die a little more so the fruit of God's compassion can grow within and around you. It could be that you need to die to your selfishness or self-centeredness, or to your need to be in control and in charge, or to your tendency to have the last word in your conversations, or to your habit of withdrawing and cutting off from others when

you are hurt, or to your attachment to reputation and status,
or to whatever else it may be that blocks God's compassion
from flowing through you to those around you. Think of one
specific way in which God may be inviting you to die daily
so that the fruit of divine compassion may grow in you.

Two Kinds of Death

Experiencing death-in-life is not an option; it's going to happen one way or another. But we get to choose which kind of death we will undergo.

First, there is the death that comes from closing our hearts to compassion. This happens when we shut them to the need around us, harden them to the human cries we hear, and live with tightly closed hands. We close the ears of our hearts to the heartbeat of the gospel, preferring to hold on to our lives rather than giving them away for the sake of the Crucified One, who gave away his life for us.

The stench of death that follows these refusals to take up the cross contaminates our relationships, families, workplaces, and public institutions. Most tragically of all, when we refuse to share in divine compassion, our own one life slowly, steadily, and surely withers away.

Second, there is the death that comes from dying to ourselves. This happens when we open our hearts to others, when we give ourselves away to others and to God, when we unclench our fists and take the hand of our neighbor.

We listen to the heartbeat of what it means to follow Jesus, choosing to lose our lives for the sake of the gospel rather than holding on to them.

While sometimes this dying can hurt like hell, it leads us into unimagined newness of life that only God can give. Our personal and public lives start smelling of a new responsiveness and aliveness that is the fruit of the divine compassion in and around us. As we learn to die, we come alive in a compassionate way to those around us. Our lives are filled with a wild, wild joy.

Which death is it going to be?

Let us choose daily to die to ourselves that we may rise into the life God wants to give us. We pray together:

Lord Jesus Christ, give me the grace to be with you in your suffering on the cross and whatever you suffer today. Free me from my tendency toward self-absorption, self-centeredness, and self-interest, so that space can be created for your compassion to flow into me and through me. Help me to freely lay down my life, with the same Spirit in which you gave up your life for me, that I may take up whatever fuller and richer life you have prepared for me. I confess that I do not find this easy. Please renew within my heart the assurance that your compassion is like a mother's womb love that will never forget me, no matter what happens. Help me now, by your Spirit, to enter your sacred mystery of dying to live, that I may bear the fruit of divine compassion toward each person in my life. May my heartbeat echo yours.

CHAPTER 7

EXPERIENCING RESURRECTION JOY

When we receive the grace of rejoicing with Jesus in his glory,
then we want to shout Alleluia over and over again.

WILLIAM BARRY

THIS SEASON OF COVID-19 has been for Debbie and me, like for countless others, a time of heartache and heartbreak. We have lamented the loss of loved ones in our extended family, our ongoing separation from our kids and our two-year-old twin grandchildren, and the immeasurable suffering caused by the virus in our beloved country. Sometimes the darkness and desolation have felt almost unbearable. Yet, the light of hope began shining again for me when, on waking up Easter Sunday this year, Debbie came into our bedroom carrying our coffee and quietly said, "Trevor, Christ is risen!" My response simply was, "He is risen indeed!"

Sometimes we live on the wrong side of Easter. When we

live as though Jesus did not rise from the grave, discipleship easily degenerates into heavyhearted efforts of trying harder to follow Jesus. This is not the *zoe* life that God wants to give us. We are not expected to love and follow Jesus into another kind of life depending on our strength of will. Rather, we are invited to join with the risen Jesus and to let his own resurrection joy and power energize us for the challenges and crises that we face every day.

This was the invitation I received again from Debbie last Easter Sunday and which I want to extend to you now.

The Significance of the Resurrection

Christians attach profound meanings to the Resurrection. To begin with, because God raised Jesus from the dead, we celebrate the truth that death has been decisively defeated. Death does not have the final word; that belongs to God (1 Corinthians 15:55). Nothing can separate us from the self-giving love of God in Christ Jesus our Lord (Romans 8:39). Nor can anything that happens to us or anything that we will ever do. Even when we are at our worst, our faithful God remains committed to our well-being, reaches out to us, and wants to live in friendship with us.

Best of all, the life that God gives—the fullness of life that Jesus proclaimed and makes possible for us—is available to every one of us. The resurrection of Jesus is God's way of being with us, in this moment, wherever we are. Through this event, the now-risen and ever-loving Christ says to each of us, "Let me breathe my Spirit into your life, that you may know I now live within you."

What is striking about the Resurrection stories in the Gospels is the absence of general statements about what the Resurrection means. Rather, the narratives simply emphasize how the disciples met with the risen Jesus, living beyond crucifixion, yet still bearing his wounds. His followers learned that he was now alive, doing what he normally did before he was killed, which was making God's love real through his presence, words, and actions.

For the disciples, the Resurrection event was not about having a theological insight; it was an encounter with the living Christ. Within a few days, these brokenhearted and dispirited disciples, whose hopes had been dashed when Jesus was put to death, were out on the streets, proclaiming the good news of the Resurrection, and they were willing to die for it.

We must ask, then: What do the Gospel writers want to tell us in these Resurrection stories?

Here is the best response I can offer: They aim to draw us into what I have called "another kind of life." Through Jesus' invisible presence, his story continues. He is the same Jesus, but he is no longer restricted by space and time. He wants to share himself with us, to speak to us, and to act in our lives. As we follow him, he emerges out of the mists of the past, becomes our ever-present Friend and Companion, and empowers us to live the *zoe* life that God gives us. The movement Jesus began rolls on right now with divine energy, joyful hope, and Resurrection aliveness, and we are invited to be part of it.

For many seekers, and certainly for me, Dallas was someone who witnessed to the realness of this ongoing Jesus story. He constantly encouraged seekers to open themselves to an encounter with the risen Jesus.

Once one of Willard's undergraduate philosophy students approached another philosophy lecturer, J. P. Moreland, and asked him, "Do you think Jesus can walk up to you?"

Recounting the conversation, Moreland says: "I asked the student, 'What do you mean by that?' And he said that he came from Dallas's office and 'he told me about Jesus,' and he said, 'Now when you pray, Jesus will walk right up to you and he will listen to you.'"[1]

For Dallas, the Resurrection was not only a theological doctrine. It was an invitation into an encounter with the living Jesus, in which we can share ourselves with him, listen to what he might say to us, and partner with him in making God's compassion more visible where we are.

The Resurrection declares that Jesus has not stopped listening, speaking, and acting. He is alive and at large in our world, in the places where we live, love, and work—and we can join him there. The Jesus story continues in you and in me!

The Joy of Jesus

I wonder whether you have any desire to explore more deeply what encountering the risen Jesus is like. When we reach the

Fourth Week of *The Spiritual Exercises*, Ignatius expects our answer will be yes.

In the Second Week, we sought to know Jesus more intimately, that we might love him more intensely and follow him more closely. In the Third Week, as we shared with the crucified Jesus in his sorrow and anguish, we asked for the gift of compassion. Now we want the risen Jesus to share the joy of his resurrection with us, as he shared it with his first disciples. As we imaginatively contemplate the Resurrected One in the Gospels, we give him the opportunity to do just this.

The Exercises were the first time I had ever asked Jesus to share his resurrection joy with me. For several reasons, it was also quite difficult.

One reason was that I did the *Spiritual Exercises* in 1990, against the backdrop of apartheid. The human suffering caused by this evil system was immeasurable. Quite frankly, I found it difficult to think of Jesus experiencing resurrection joy while millions around me were suffering from oppression. To do so would have seemed to strengthen the already prevalent idea among those who were oppressed that Jesus did not really care about their situation. It felt more appropriate to stay in the Third Week, which was focused on the suffering of Jesus, in both his crucifixion and in those who were suffering around me.

Another reason was that I did not rate high on the joy meter myself. Not only did the senselessness of the suffering around me take me to dark places in my own heart but my own temperament was constantly characterized by dissatisfaction, discontent, and dejection. Those closest to me, especially Debbie, my partner in marriage, would often express concern about my frequent bouts of spiritual heaviness and downheartedness. Joy was a stranger in my life.

Then—and this is harder to admit—I found my ingrained tendency toward self-absorption again rearing its head. It did not come easy for me, especially if I was feeling down and gloomy, to participate freely in someone else's joy.

Given that I could not make myself share in someone else's joy, asking for the grace of the Fourth Week became essential. I had to ask Jesus to open my heart to his resurrection joy. He needed to help me to do what I could not do in my own strength.

These were some of the reasons why I struggled to share in the joy of the risen Jesus. My journal entries from that time of doing the Exercises remind me that it was a gradual journey. Here are some sentences lifted from the daily reviews that I did as I prayed imaginatively with the Resurrection narratives during the Fourth Week:

- "I felt tired today when I came to the empty tomb. I do not sense Jesus' joyful risen presence."
- "It was a struggle to be in the garden with Mary. My mind was all over the place."
- "I heard Jesus calling my name to turn away from my preoccupations and my busyness and toward him."
- "I shared with Jesus my longing to participate in his joy."

- "As I had breakfast with the risen Jesus and his disciples, I saw joy in his eyes."

This journey into the joy of the risen Jesus has deepened over the past thirty years. It was helpful to have witnessed this radiant joy in Dallas's life. Although he was no stranger to suffering, he radiated joy. Whether I listened to him hum a favorite hymn or caught him in his room delighting in photographs of his family, stood quietly with him as the sun set over a lake or enjoyed a beer and spicy chicken after a long day of ministry, or even watched him struggle with virulent cancer, I felt a contagious joy about his presence.

In one significant conversation, soon after I had done the Exercises, he gently challenged me to keep asking the risen Jesus for the gift of his joy. Slowly, the Stranger became a good Friend, and he remains so today, even in difficult and dark times.

SEEKING EXERCISE

Would you like to share in the joy of the risen Jesus? You may want to put this book down and think about your response for a few moments.

If your answer is yes, Ignatius would invite you to express this desire directly in prayer: "Lord, please reveal your resurrection joy to me so I can share it with you."

*Then he would say something like "Now give the risen
Lord an opportunity to come to you. Read a Gospel
story of Jesus appearing to his disciples. Step into it
as imaginatively as you are able, engage with the risen
Jesus, and ask him to reveal his joy to you. Pay special
attention to the way he consoled and comforted his
disciples, for that is how he still comes to us today."*

Resurrection Encounters with Jesus

If I had to spend time alone in an isolated place, and you allowed me to take just one portion of Scripture with me, I would choose one of the resurrection stories of Jesus. They have become close companions. Most especially, they have encouraged me to be more aware of the hidden presence of the joyful Christ in the ordinary moments of my life.

In my early Christ-following days, when listening to others describe how Christ had come to them, I would often think, *I wish that had happened for me.* There was usually something dramatic, out-of-the-ordinary, and spectacular about their testimonies, whereas most of my life seemed much more humdrum and mundane. As a result, I felt that I was missing out on encountering the risen Jesus. Thankfully, as I have lived with these Resurrection stories, they have encouraged me to recognize how Christ also encounters us in the ordinary and menial.

I hope that I can encourage you to discover the presence of Christ in the unspectacular details of your daily life. To help with this task of recognition, with Ignatius and Dallas as our companions, let us reflect on three common features of the Resurrection stories.[2] As we keep one foot in our imaginative contemplation of the Gospel narratives, and the other foot in our everyday realities, we will notice how the risen Jesus slips into our lives.

In his foreword for a book I wrote about Mary's encounter with the Resurrected One, Dallas pointed out just how quietly and unobtrusively this happens.

> [These] stories of Jesus are the primary overtures of grace in a world that knows little of true gift. We can let them in. Indeed, they are so winsome, who can keep them out once they appear? They are like raindrops and sunshine, and the flowers in our soul begin to grow. Without our knowing how, without our even intending it. We begin to find good we did not expect or hope for: here, there, in the world, in others. In ourselves, can it be? We ask, "Who has done this?" And we find that Jesus himself came in with the stories.[3]

This is my prayer as you read on, that, as we reflect on these common features of the Resurrection stories, we will notice the living presence of Jesus in and around us with a fresh sensitivity.

At the End of Our Rope

The first common feature of the Resurrection stories is that those to whom the risen Jesus came were at the end of their rope. Mary was weeping in the garden, overcome by her grief. The two pilgrims who walked along the Emmaus Road, their faces downcast, were saying, "We had hoped . . ." Thomas was battling with crippling doubt and terrible disappointment. The disciples were in lockdown because of their fear. Peter was struggling with haunting memories of failure and betrayal. Small wonder that Dallas would sometimes say that "Jesus' address in our lives is endoftherope.com." This was certainly his address in the lives of his first disciples.

Notice that, in each of these Resurrection encounters, the risen Jesus came looking for his followers. The searching Christ reminds us that at the heart of this universe, there is a Great Love who longs for our friendship. Even when we have wandered far away from divine friendship, God continually seeks us out, just as Jesus sought out his disciples and friends after his resurrection. The divine Lover never lets us go, nor does he ever give up on us. God wants to find us so that we may find the answer to our deepest desires and longings. Our seeking after God is simply a faint echo of this seeking love of God, so powerfully revealed in the Resurrection stories.

When Jesus sought out those at the end of their rope, he always came as the Consoler, and in a way that was uniquely relevant for each person. The consolation he shared was not superficial or clichéd. Jesus didn't say, "Cheer up! Can't you see it's Easter Sunday morning? Put a smile on your face, and let's get on with life." Rather, as he comforted them through his risen presence, his life-giving words, and his loving actions, the effect of this consolation on his followers was inward.

Their hearts began to burn again with reignited faith, hope, and love. While they still had to face hostile circumstances, and would undergo much more suffering, they knew that their crucified and risen Friend was now with them in a new and different way. This made all the difference.

What does this mean for us?

There are many ways in which we come to the end of our rope. We get struck down by illness, a loved one dies, the person we love does not love us, we ache for children living far away, we struggle with chronic pain, we wrestle with a despairing darkness, we battle to break free from an addiction, we get old on our own, or _____ (insert your own experience here). These painful moments become moments of encounter with the risen Christ as we bring our pain to him, tell him about it, and then give him the space to reveal himself to us.

Just as he consoled his first followers, so he also consoles us with his presence, his words, and his actions. When he does, our hearts begin to burn again with faith, hope, and love—just like those early disciples.

A few weeks ago, I had a major disappointment, and for a few days I could not get the incident out of my mind. Whenever I thought about it, my heart felt heavy and sad.

One morning, on my usual early morning run, I shared

my disappointment with Jesus like those Emmaus pilgrims did. For about ten minutes, I endeavored to put my feelings into words.

About half an hour afterward, as I continued running, a thought surprised me. It was simple and straightforward: *Lay it down, Trevor.*

My immediate question was whether this was my own thought or whether it was the Lord speaking to me.

Because of its quiet authority, and its consoling effect on my heart, I chose to believe that Christ had prompted this thought. Since then, I have been asking Jesus to help me let go of this disappointment and trust him with my future. As each day passes, I find a greater freedom and sense of joyful release about this matter.

SEEKING EXERCISE

Right now, I invite you to do something similar. Let me ask: With whom do you identify the most in the Resurrection stories? Is it with Mary and her tears, the Emmaus Road pilgrims in their disappointment and hopelessness, Thomas with his doubt, the disciples in their fear, or Peter in his failure? In what way do you feel you are at the end of your rope?

Read whichever Gospel story is most apt for you, and picture yourself participating in it. Share with Christ, as fully as you are able, your feelings and

*thoughts. Invite him to reveal his risen presence to
you and come to you in whatever way he chooses.*

*After your time of conversational prayer, reflect on your time
with him. Then continue to go about life as usual, with a
quiet sense of expectancy that he will come to you. My prayer
is that you will experience the consolation of Jesus' living
presence, just as his friends in the Resurrection stories did.*

————————

Gradual Recognition

The second common feature of the Resurrection stories is
the gradual recognition of the risen Jesus by his disciples and
friends. None of them recognized him immediately. Mary
initially thought he was the gardener. Only after he spoke
her name did she recognize him. The Emmaus Road pilgrims
realized, hours after their conversation with the stranger, that
their hearts had burned within them when he had spoken
with them. At first the disciples who had gone fishing did
not recognize Jesus when he stood on the shore. It was only
after they had acted on his words to throw their nets on the
right side of the boat and caught many fish that they realized
it was the risen Lord who had spoken to them. Recognizing
the consoling presence of the risen Christ happened gradually for these early Christ followers.

To explore this feature of gradual recognition, let us step
imaginatively into the story of the risen Jesus' encounter with

the Emmaus Road pilgrims (Luke 24:13-35). This Gospel story serves as a helpful model of the gradual way we come to know the presence of Christ in our lives.

On that terrible Friday when Jesus was crucified, the hopes of these two pilgrims had been shattered. They had regarded Jesus as a prophet, and even more than a prophet. They had thought he was God's Messiah who would liberate their people. But now the one on whom they had pinned their hopes was dead and gone. When the Stranger who joined them on the road and asked them what things they were talking about as they walked along, they explained, "The things about Jesus of Nazareth, who was a prophet mighty in deed and word before God and all the people, and how our chief priests and leaders handed him over to be condemned to death and crucified him. But we had hoped that he was the one to redeem Israel" (Luke 24:19-21).

On Sunday morning they had heard that some women had found the tomb empty, but they decided to leave Jerusalem and walk home. They were devastated, not only because Jesus had been killed but also because, as the one whom God had chosen, he should have defeated the Romans rather than died at their hands.

Picture now their encounter with the risen Jesus. As the two travelers walk along the road, a stranger joins them. They do not initially recognize that this person is Jesus. When he asks them about their downcast faces, they share their broken hopes. Listen as they pour out their feelings of sadness, disappointment, and despair. Notice how the stranger pays attention to them. Sense their gratitude for the willingness of this stranger to listen so intently to their story. It must have helped these two grief-stricken pilgrims to unload their pain with another person in this way. Recall a time when someone has listened to the story of your heartache and heartbreak. It may help you to get some sense of what it was like for them to share their hearts with this listening stranger.

At this point in the story, there comes a sudden change. The stranger breaks into the conversation, almost rudely. He takes them through the Scriptures and explains that the Messiah had to suffer. Their hearts burn as he explains these things to them. They know of only one person who can speak like this, and he is dead.

This stranger who is speaking to them has the same understanding of the Scriptures that Jesus had when they were with him. He had taught them about how God would liberate his people through the suffering of his servant: "Was it not necessary that the Messiah should suffer these things and then enter into his glory?" (Luke 24:26). This was the way God had intended to fulfill his purposes in the world, and now he had done just that. Still, they do not recognize Jesus.

When they come to the fork in the road, the pilgrims do not want to let the stranger go. They beg him to come home with them. The stranger responds to their urgings and accompanies them to their home.

At suppertime, when he breaks the bread, "their eyes were opened, and they recognized him; and he vanished from their sight" (Luke 24:31). Their recognition, however, goes even deeper than this. They ask each other, "Were not our hearts burning within us while he was talking to us on the road, while he was opening the scriptures to us?" (verse 32).

As you have imagined this encounter and interacted with it, I wonder what your reactions have been. You may want to share them with the risen Christ right now.

Let me tease out some threads of the pilgrims' gradual recognition of Jesus.

When Jesus came alongside them, they did not at first recognize him. Even when their hearts burned as he spoke to them, they still did not realize that it was Jesus. But they did take seriously their feelings of being drawn toward this stranger. Significantly, had they failed to act on this attraction, they would have not recognized the risen Jesus.

Later, when they sat down to supper, the moment of recognition occurred. They recognized Jesus as he took bread and broke it in his usual manner. This recognition became stronger when they connected their heart-burning moment with the characteristic consoling effects of Jesus' presence and words on their hearts, as they had known it before. Whenever Jesus had been with them, he had caused their hearts to burn with faith, hope, and love. Now it had happened again.

This feature of gradual recognition gets confirmed in our own personal encounters with the risen Christ. When he comforts us in our grief and loss, gives us hope in our hopelessness, transmits peace in our fear, encourages faith in our wrestling with doubt, offers guidance when we don't know what to do, renews our personal calling when we let him down, we usually don't recognize him immediately. Most often, it is as we become aware of certain inner movements of our heart that the truth gradually dawns: *Yes, it was Christ who was with us.* For this reason, like the Emmaus pilgrims, we need to pay attention to those times when our hearts burn. Then we also need to invite the stranger home with us, let him explain the Scriptures to us, and listen to what he may be saying to us.

Later, we will see how Ignatius offers us practical guidelines that help us recognize the presence of Christ through his distinctive consoling effects on our heart.

Commissioned for Ministry

A third common feature of the Resurrection stories is that those to whom the risen Christ came were commissioned for ministry. Not one of them sat back complacently after their Resurrection encounter and said, "Christ is risen! Death has been conquered. My sins have been forgiven. Now I can do nothing because I am on my way to heaven." Each one knew that they had gospel work to do in this broken world.

- Jesus told Mary to go immediately to the rest of the disciples and to tell them the good news (John 20:17).

- The Emmaus pilgrims got up from their meal with Jesus and returned to Jerusalem to share what had happened to them (Luke 24:33-35).

- For the disciples behind locked doors, Jesus breathed his Spirit into them with the words "As the Father has sent me, so I send you" (John 20:21).

- After Jesus asked Peter whether he loved Jesus, Jesus called Peter to be a shepherd to the flock with the instruction "Feed my sheep" (John 21:17).

To be encountered by the risen Jesus is to become part of an Easter people living in a Good Friday world.[4] Like those first Christ followers, we are also summoned to become God's agents of Resurrection newness, and to bring God's compassion and consolation to those around us, especially the most vulnerable. As Jesus' friends, we seek to do this as he would, if he were in our place. Like him, we are called to listen to those who weep, walk alongside the hopeless, be with the frightened, engage the doubt filled, shepherd the hurting, bless the brokenhearted, and announce the availability of another kind of life to those who have not heard. Each of us has a unique role to fulfill in Jesus' ministry of making God's healing love real in our world.

Dallas was one such agent of Resurrection newness. Here are the words of a colleague and a gifted musician, Reverend Rowan Rogers, describing a meeting with Dallas in the late 1990s, when Rowan was at the end of his rope.

Much like the friends who lowered a paralyzed man through the roof of the house, to the feet of Jesus, a few people "conspired" to get me to spend an afternoon with Dallas Willard. They knew my life was in trouble, and someone thought that I might benefit from a conversation with Dallas. I knew a little about Dallas, but not enough to care whether I saw him or not. Nevertheless, I agreed to go, unaware at the time of the immense privilege.

Dallas welcomed me warmly and asked to hear my story. I had come prepared with a long list of grievances against others, God, and myself—but mostly against the uncaring nature of God. As I told my story, of how I had hurt others, and of how God did not seem to care, Dallas listened. And every now and then he would interject with grace-filled questions. As I was sharing one particularly painful story, he spoke words of such kindness, mercy, and grace. He spoke with a gentle, priestly authority, which allowed me to hear the whisper of the Spirit: "Your sins are forgiven, all of them." (Even as I write these words, tears still come.)

Our meeting concluded with a transforming blessing. Dallas had listened patiently to my rantings against the God who ignores and who favors discriminately. He asked if I might do this one thing as we parted. He said something like: "Are you willing to see everything that is good as being a gift from God; and everything that is not good as not being from God?"

Within two weeks of our meeting, I was a transformed human being—still in need of great grace, but back on my feet, and beginning the gentle journey home. It remains the single greatest turning point of my life.[5]

SEEKING EXERCISE

How is the risen Lord calling you to bring consolation to those around you?

We cannot take on all the pain and misery around us. We cannot wipe away all the tears, care for all the destitute, get alongside all the sick, befriend all the lonely, empower all the poor. But we can take time to be with the Lord and to ask him, "Which human cry touches my heart the most? Toward whom do I feel a sense of compassion rising within me? What little piece of your dream for the healing of this world are you inviting me to make real?" Take some time to consider these questions in relation to your own life.

When we ask questions like these, listen to the inner movements of our own hearts, notice those stirrings of compassion that rise within us, and follow them up with thoughtful actions, we begin to live as an Easter people in a Good Friday world.

_____

Recognizing Consolation

The risen Christ encounters us in many ways, not only through the Gospel stories. As Paul reminds us, the presence of the resurrected and ascended Christ now fills the universe (Ephesians 4:10). His loving and consoling presence is no longer localized in one geographical spot. His living presence is now freely and infinitely available to every human being, everywhere, through all time. He wants to meet us, wherever we are, whatever we are doing, and whoever we are with. It is especially within our everyday lives—cooking meals, playing with the children, cleaning the house, going to work, enjoying our friendships—that he comes to us. This is where we experience his consoling presence within us. Our task is to recognize that presence and respond to it.

Remember our earlier learning from the burning hearts of the Emmaus pilgrims? We recognize the risen Lord's consoling presence through the inner movements of our heart. One of Ignatius's special gifts to the church was his "Rules for the Discernment of Spirits." He knew that the human heart consists of many different impulses, feelings, moods, daydreams, desires, and so on. These complex and highly individual inward experiences accompany us wherever we go. The genius of Ignatius was to provide guidelines that can help us distinguish between those inner effects that indicate the presence of Christ speaking and acting in our lives, and those that do not.

An exhaustive study of these rules lies outside the scope

of this book, but I want to simplify some of them into a few homely guidelines that we can apply to our lives. In doing this, I am assuming that the core of your being is oriented toward God and that you deeply desire to follow Christ. Let me assure you that if you are worried whether this is true for you, it is a sign that you are seeking God's way and will for your life. If it were not, as Gerard Hughes points out, you would not be worried![6]

Ignatius offered two broad categories for identifying these inner movements of our heart: *spiritual consolation* and *spiritual desolation*.

By spiritual consolation, Ignatius was not necessarily referring to the natural feel-good factor we get when everything goes along without a hitch. The consolation that Ignatius wanted us to identify is a "spiritual" consolation. This is a movement of the Spirit within our heart that draws us toward God. This does not mean it cannot be related to our natural positive feelings; often spiritual consolation and natural consolation go together. But spiritual consolation can also be experienced in times of great struggle and can include both pleasant and painful feelings and thoughts.[7]

Second, Ignatius described the inner state of spiritual consolation in the following way: It refers to any burning desire for God, to tears that come for our sin that breaks the heart of God, or to a feeling of empathy for the suffering of Jesus or for any other suffering person. It involves every increase in faith, hope, and love that takes place within us, and a deep-down sense of peace.[8] Paul described the fruit of the Spirit as "love, joy, peace, patience, kindness, generosity, faithfulness, gentleness, and self-control" (Galatians 5:22-23). When we experience these kinds of inner movements in our heart, we can be reasonably sure that we are being moved by the Spirit of the risen Christ.

Spiritual desolation, Ignatius made clear, is the opposite of this. It refers to those inner states when we are filled with thoughts of rebelliousness toward God, despair, and selfishness. It is those inner movements of the heart that draw us away from faith, hope, and love. We are in spiritual desolation when we "find ourselves enmeshed in a certain turmoil of spirit or feel ourselves weighed down by a heavy darkness or weight."9 Generally, these kinds of inner movements are not prompted by the Spirit of Christ.

It follows from these contrasting descriptions of spiritual consolation and spiritual desolation that when we are in a time of spiritual desolation, it would be unwise to go back on a decision that we made in a time of spiritual consolation. The reason is that the thoughts and choices that spring from desolation are different from those that originate in consolation. They are not prompted by the Spirit of God. Rather, we should face our desolation, talk about it with someone we trust, examine its causes, and make decisions that act against it. Times of spiritual desolation come to all of us from time to time, and even when we cannot discern what brought it on, we can ask God to help us to stay faithful in our desolation until spiritual consolation returns.

As I write, we are in our second year of a national lockdown because of COVID-19. It has been a strange, challenging, and worrying time. On the day after Easter Sunday this year, Debbie and I sat together and reflected on those moments that have brought us spiritual consolation. We asked ourselves: *When did we sense an increase in faith, hope, and love?* The top five times that we identified were moments of closeness between the two of us, our daily walks with the dogs within our complex; our video calls with our children (who are overseas); our enjoyment of the beauty in the garden; and lighting a candle at suppertime, when we spend about five minutes in silence together. In these ordinary moments of consolation, the risen Christ touched our lives.

SEEKING EXERCISE

Make a list of five moments of spiritual consolation in your life during these past few days. Remember they do not have to be spectacular or dramatic; they can be down-to-earth and simple. As we have seen, our natural moments can become the springboard for our experience of the risen Christ's consoling presence in our lives. Write a paragraph about each of them. As you savor them and allow them more space in your heart and mind, how do you sense the Spirit inviting you into the future?

An Easter People in a Good Friday World

These reflections on the inner movements of our heart are not intended to turn our attention away from the world. After all, at the heart of Jesus' good news is the availability of another kind of life. This fullness of life from God is a resurrection life of unimagined newness, in which we are consoled by the risen Christ and commissioned to make God's love more real, wherever we are. We do this as we share the compassion and consolation that we have received from the crucified and risen Jesus. We become an Easter people in a Good Friday world.

Our "burning heart" moments remind us that in this consoling and compassionate ministry, we are not alone. The living Lord is with us, and as he encounters us along the way, his presence with us is turned into an intimate friendship that goes far beyond what we have known before.

I invite you to pray with me.

Lord Jesus Christ, your risen and ascended presence fills this universe. You meet us wherever we are, especially when we are at the end our rope. Thank you for the quiet, hidden, and unobtrusive way you come to us. Thank you for how you touch our lives in those special

*moments that we call consolation. Thank you
for those times when you come alongside us and
make our hearts burn with new faith, hope,
and love. Help us not to keep your consoling
presence for ourselves. Help us, rather, to
allow these times of spiritual consolation to
lead us into deeper faithfulness, that we may
bring your compassion and consolation to
others. Help us to know, with a renewed sense
of assurance, that you are always with us.
Please be our resurrection and our life.*

CHAPTER 8

FINDING GOD IN ALL THINGS

—

To [Jesus'] eyes, this is a God-bathed and God-permeated world.

DALLAS WILLARD

AT THE BEGINNING OF THIS BOOK, I invited you to become a seeker. This invitation continues. It does not grow old, become irrelevant, or get stale. When it comes to our spiritual journey, we can never say that we have "arrived." The attitude and action of continual seeking expresses God's hope for us. Ponder one more time these words from Jeremiah: "When you search for me, you will find me; if you seek me with all your heart, I will let you find me, says the LORD" (Jeremiah 29:13-14).

Our seeking has been focused on the biblical vision of another kind of life. Remember those five interwoven threads that characterize the tapestry of this new life Jesus has made freely available:

1. deepening intimacy with God;
2. growing belonging within God's family;
3. gradual transformation into compassionate image bearers;
4. reception of power from beyond ourselves; and
5. an inner assurance that we are held safe in God's love forever.

I pray and hope that, as you have sought this other kind of life, these threads have become more real in your own experience.

Our seeking journey has been shaped by the structure of the *Spiritual Exercises*. Each of the themes of the Four Weeks has guided us. Our journey began as we came to know that we are deeply loved sinners. We entered through the doorway of repentance, then continued along its pathway. We took time to discern our deepest desires. We asked to know Jesus more deeply, so that we would love him more intensely and follow him more closely. We embraced the sacred mystery of dying to live. We shared in the joy of the risen Christ, opened our hearts to his consoling presence, and received his commission to be agents of his consolation in our hurting world.

We never fully exhaust any of these themes; rather, as we continuously seek God, we come back to them over and over. The reason is that, at different times in our relationship with

God, different desires and longings emerge within us. What we are seeking determines which theme will be most relevant for us at that time.

My desire to share in the resurrection joy of Jesus stayed with me long after I had finished the Exercises. This meant that I continued asking to share in Jesus' present joy. At this moment, as I desire to follow Jesus more closely in my aging years, the Second Week theme of discipleship has again connected powerfully. Once more I am contemplating the Gospel stories, seeking to know Jesus better as he reveals himself to me within those diminishments that come as I age.

SEEKING EXERCISE

Take a few moments to reflect on your own seeking journey again. In the light of our journey together through this book, what do you desire most right now in your relationship with God? You may want to know God's personal love more deeply, or experience God's forgiveness for recent failures, or discern your deepest longings, or get to know Jesus better, or be closer to him in his passion, or share in his resurrection joy. It could be helpful to write this desire down before reading further.

As one nears the end of the Exercises, Ignatius assumes that the retreatant will want to love and serve God with their whole life. This desire may resonate with you as we conclude our journey together. If it does, you will find the last structured contemplation in the Exercises particularly helpful.

Contemplating the Love of God

In the final prayer exercise, Ignatius invites us to contemplate the immeasurable depths of God's self-giving love and respond with everything that we have and are. He does this in a way that is inviting, grace filled, and down-to-earth. Before he presents the exercise, Ignatius says two critical things about how love is expressed. Clearly, he wanted us to know what he meant when he used the word.

First, he said, "Love ought to show itself in deeds over and above words."[1] While he did not say that love cannot be expressed in words, Ignatius believed that love reveals itself most authentically in acts of compassionate service. Practicality was important for him.

Second, he observed that "love consists of a mutual sharing of goods."[2] William Barry points out just how extraordinary and breathtaking this statement is: Ignatius presupposed that the God who needs nothing, who creates us out of love and not necessity, wants complete mutuality with us. Barry writes, "God wants to be our dearest friend, our tremendous lover, and our beloved. . . . If I do not choose to respond in mutuality, then God cannot be for me who God wants to be; namely my beloved."[3]

I want now to adapt this exercise so that you can go through it with me. Once we have done this, I would like to offer a reflection on this prayer exercise, which will hopefully take us to the heart of Ignatius's faith vision.

Ever since I did this exercise for the first time, this way of understanding how God relates to our world has significantly shaped my own seeking journey. It also guides how I encourage others to seek God. I hope that it will become a guidepost for you as you continue to seek the life that God offers.

As we begin, decide on a place where you will not be interrupted and where you can speak aloud to God. Set aside a block of time to do this exercise. Please do not feel that you must finish this exercise in one session. You can spread it over a few days. It needs to be an unhurried, relaxed time with God.

When you are alone, take time to settle down, and remind yourself that God is looking at you with overwhelming love and affirmation. Ignatius suggests that, as you begin this prayer exercise, you ask God for what you want in these words: "Lord, please give me a deeply felt knowledge of all your goodness toward me, so that, stirred with great gratitude, I may become able to love you and serve you in all things."[4]

From the First Week onward, Ignatius assumes that the person doing the Exercises has a clear sense of God's personal love. Now he wants them to grow into a more passionate, wholehearted, and fiercer love for God. Remember, too, that Ignatius wanted this exercise to be a *contemplation* of God's love, something that we enter with all our imaginative senses, not just with our rational mind.

First, remember gifts from God you have received.

Begin by asking God to help you recall those gifts that have made divine love real for you. This is a time to let memories of the special people you have known fill you with a heart-felt sense of gratitude and thankfulness. You could begin by remembering your childhood, parents, family, teachers, mentors, colleagues, and friends. Throughout your life, God has been present and loving you through those who have cared for you and looked after you. Picture these significant moments when you have felt loved, cherished, and valued, and hold them in your memory for a while.

In addition to these gifts, there is the gift of how God has personally reached out to you and drawn you into relationship with Jesus Christ. Right from the beginning of your existence, God has been wooing you, growing your desire for divine friendship, attracting you into an intimate relationship. Ask the Lord to show you how his Spirit has helped you respond to these divine initiatives and promptings. Remind yourself again that all your seeking for God is just a faint echo of how much God's wholehearted and sacrificial love continually seeks you.

You can also give thanks for whatever gifts you may have received while reading this book. It may have been a helpful insight, a new awareness, or a fresh understanding. You may have found yourself experiencing more deeply some aspect of the life that God offers. This might be a positive difference in your relationship with God, a greater connection with your sisters and brothers in God's family, a clearer sense of how God is calling you at this time, a growing compassion for those around you, a stronger appreciation of God's power within you, or a deepening assurance that nothing can stand between you and God's love, revealed in Jesus Christ.

As you recall the gifts that you have received, what thoughts and feelings do you have? You may want to express them by saying the challenging prayer that Ignatius gives in this exercise. It is commonly called "Take, Lord, and Receive," and it goes like this:

> Take, Lord, and receive all my liberty, my memory, my understanding, and all my will—all that I have and possess. You, Lord, have given all that to me. I now give it back to you, O Lord. All of it is yours. Dispose of it according to your will. Give me love of yourself along with grace, for that is enough for me.[5]

This prayer stretches us to the limit of what it means to love God. It reminds us that the seeking journey never ends.

I do not believe I have ever been able to say it and mean it completely. Sometimes, to be honest, I am unsure whether God's grace and love is enough for me. I do, however, genuinely want this to be true for me. I know that the joyful freedom of being able to abandon myself in love and service will come only with this complete self-surrender.

"Lord, help me want to know that your love and grace is enough for me," is my oft-repeated prayer, "that I may be set free to trust you with all of my life." It takes time to love God with the whole of our being.

Second, notice how God dwells in everything that God has created.

Ignatius here invites you to imagine God's intimate presence in everything around you. At this point, you may want to take a walk outside and gaze at what surrounds you. Imagine God present in the flowers, the clouds, the sky, the trees, the insects, the grass. Imagine, also, God present in the people you see (those whom you love, those who live next door, those you do not like) and in your own life as well.

Here we let the magnificent words of Paul in the New Testament—"there is . . . one God and Father of all, who is above all and through all and in all"—become tangible in all that we can see, touch, hear, taste, and smell (Ephesians 4:6). Celebrate the astonishing reality that we can encounter the invisible one in all things visible.

If you are in a place of extreme pain and great loss right now, being able to see God's presence in everything around you may not be easy. The invitation to do so may evoke strong feelings of anger and resistance. Should this be where you are, then as you read these words, Ignatius would gently encourage you to ask again for what you desire: "Lord, please give me a deeply felt knowledge of all your goodness toward me, so that, stirred with great gratitude, I may become able to love you and serve you in all things."[6]

Ignatius knew from the ups and downs of his own life just

how differently our world looks when viewed from the experience of chronic pain, grief, and desperate disappointment. In these difficult moments we cannot just manufacture the attitude that sees God in everything; rather, we need to ask God to please renew our faith so that we can.

As you contemplate God's love in everything around you, pay attention to what you feel and think. Share your thoughts and feelings with God, especially if this was difficult for you. How do you sense God respond to what you have been asking for in this exercise? Do you have a greater awareness of God's loving goodness toward you?

You may feel able to express the response of your heart to God right now as you pray again, "Take, Lord, and receive . . ."

Third, imagine God working creatively on your behalf in everything around you.

Ignatius was convinced that God is always working for our good and for the good of the world. As Paul wrote, "We know that in all things God works for the good of those who love him, who have been called according to his purpose" (Romans 8:28, NIV).

In his third point, Ignatius invites us to shift our imagination from a static image of God's loving presence to the dynamic image of God continually creating everything around us on our behalf.[7] He wants us to imagine God's creative activities going on all the time, in every particle of creation, for our sake and the sake of the world.

The Spirit of God is always at work in our world, with

the promise that God will bring something beautiful out of the chaos and confusion. Set your imagination free to imagine God's creative activity happening around you, so that you can be drawn into the other kind of life that God wants to give you.

You may also want to imagine God's ongoing active presence in your own life. The psalmist reminds us that God formed our inward parts and knit us together in our mother's womb (Psalm 139:13).

Ignatius would want us to know that God has not put these knitting needles down. In this moment God continues to be at work in you, and in all the experiences, encounters, and events of your life, with the intention of bringing you more fully into that divine friendship for which your heart longs. You are never abandoned to find your way home on your own. Picture, in whatever way you are able, God's creative activity in your unfolding life, especially how it is making itself known in what you most deeply desire.

As you contemplate God working creatively on your behalf, how do you respond? Would you like to be part of God's ongoing creative activity in our world and in your own life? Do you want to love and serve God in all your conversations, relationships, work, leisure, and everyday activities?

Should there be a *Yes* in your heart, focus your desire as you pray, "Take, Lord, and receive . . ."

Fourth, receive God's love in every good gift you enjoy.

Finally, Ignatius invites us to imagine God loving us in all the good gifts we enjoy. He wants us to know that, as James points out, just as the sunshine rays come from the sun, every good gift descends from God (James 1:17).

How do we understand this image of comparing God's love to the sun and sunshine? It is the nature of the sun always to radiate warmth and light. Whatever we do, it cannot act against its essential nature. Likewise, God always loves. In every moment of our life, God continuously sends out warm rays of divine love to us. We cannot stop God loving us.

Imagine how this happens each day in the ordinary moments of your everyday life. Throughout the day, God's love comes to you in every good gift you receive. It comes in the sun that warms you, the water you drink, the food you eat, the energy you use, the friend who hugs you, the stranger who greets you—indeed in your very existence. You can consciously receive God's love as you inhale the air you breathe, or feel the light of the sun on your face, or wash your hands with water, or delight in the life you now live.

How do you respond to the warmth of the sunshine of God's love shining in every gift you receive? As you come to the end of this prayer exercise, what dominant thoughts and feelings rise within you?

In response to all that God has given you, and continues to give you, you may want to offer again, with all the love and longing of your heart, the prayer "Take, Lord, and receive . . ."

Reimagining Our World

Contemplating God's love like this, during the *Spiritual Exercises*, helped me imagine our world differently. If you asked me to describe this difference, I would put it like this: *My eyes were opened to see that God could be sought and found everywhere.*

I failed to grasp this truth in the early days of my walk with God. Everyday life seemed separated into strict "spiritual" and "unspiritual" compartments. There was the sacred space of prayer, Bible reading, worship, meeting for fellowship, and other church-related activities where I expected God to be. Then there was the secular space—those routine, ordinary parts of the daily grind in our families, jobs, leisure times—where I thought God would not be. Every time a well-meaning preacher encouraged me "to take Christ into the world" (where he was supposedly not present and active), this split spirituality was deepened.[8]

Gradually, it dawned on me that the people in the Bible saw things differently. Repeatedly, the Scriptures bear witness to the presence of God being encountered everywhere and in everything.

- In his temple vision of the Lord seated high upon the throne of heaven, Isaiah wrote of the seraphim, in the divine presence, calling out to each other, "Holy, holy, holy is the LORD of hosts; the whole earth is full of his glory" (Isaiah 6:3).

- Preaching to the Athenians, Paul declared boldly that God is always near, for "in him we live and move and have our being" (Acts 17:28).

- In the closing moments of his earthly ministry, Jesus assured his disciples that they would always be accompanied by his risen presence. "And remember," he said to them on the mountain in Galilee, "I am with you always, to the end of the age" (Matthew 28:20).

When I imagined God's love in the four ways that Ignatius suggested, these biblical verses moved from my head to my heart. Not only did my theology change but I started to seek God's active presence in areas of my life where I had not sought the divine presence before. The split in my spirituality began to be healed as I recognized that there was no part of my life where God was not present and active. As a result, the good news that we can find God wherever we are began to sink into my heart. Now I saw why Ignatius would say to his companions that they "can practice seeking the presence of our Lord in all things—in their dealings with other people, their walking, seeing, tasting, hearing, understanding, and in all our actions.—For his Divine Majesty truly is in everything by his presence, power, and essence."[9]

SEEKING EXERCISE

Before we explore further how we can experience this faith vision of finding God in all things, take a moment to identify the areas of split spirituality that you experience in yourself.

One way to do this is to think about what you seldom or never talk to God about. It could be your sexuality, your anger, your pain, your fear, your resentment, your longings.

We often do not share with God those feelings that cause us discomfort or embarrassment. An inner split develops between our spiritual and emotional lives. Sometimes our lack of compassion, our use of financial resources, or our views about violence reveals a clear division between our faith and our social lives. Healing the faith-life fractures in our life with God usually begins when we identify what they are and talk with God about them.

As you identify these splits in your spirituality, bring them before the Lord and share them with him.

Experiencing God in All Things

How do we begin to experience God in all things? One way of doing this consists of identifying sources of enjoyment and believing that God is lovingly present within them.

As I have already shared, for many years I lived with a pervasive sense of discontent and disappointment. During the Fourth Week of the *Spiritual Exercises*, when I asked to share in the joy of the risen Jesus, this began to change.

I wrote to Dallas and shared with him what was happening in my slow journey toward joy. I received a letter back with realistic and practical direction. Not only did his response indicate a kind acceptance of who I was but it also offered some clues regarding what I could do to enjoy and experience God more in the whole of my life. Here are parts of his response.

> Being discontent and always halfway disappointed is a part of what *you* are as a pilgrim on this earth. You are always going to feel that "arrangements," whether family, church, or state, are sawdust and not bread. Most likely, it derives from something—not bad— in your early experiences that formed your feelings and sentiment and left a gap in your sensitivities. Something it would take a revelation from God to make you know and which you could do nothing about if you did know. Introspectiveness is part of your nature. It is not bad. Do not fight it. Find sources of joy and cultivate them. Invest in them: time and money. . . . What things do you really enjoy? Things that have nothing to do with family, work, or religion. I want you to write me about three sources of pure joy that you know from your own experience. . . . There is a kind of infinity in the sensibility of the human soul, and it imposes great burdens and temptations.[10]

I frequently return to these words. They have helped me see how I can live in a way more conducive to experiencing and enjoying God's joy in all things. Dallas's words encouraged me to experience and enjoy God in the gift of my own existence. Being discontent and introspective does not mean that God has done badly by me, or that there is something wrong with me, or that I am inferior in any way. So, over the years, I have been asking for the grace to know more deeply that when God looks at me, God says, "Trevor, I did good in creating you. Feel my delight in your existence. I continue to breathe life into you. I dwell in you. Know that you make me smile."

Dallas's counsel was intriguingly "unspiritual." There was no word about praying, studying the Bible, or praising God more. I knew that these activities were important to him, but his approach to my struggles was based on the conviction that God could be experienced in all things, especially those things that we enjoyed. I did not have to fill my conversation with religious expressions of praise and thanksgiving all day long. What I could do was appreciate this present moment of my life, enjoy it as deeply as I could, and experience God's creative goodness in it.

After all, as Gerard Hughes has observed, "if you have prepared a meal, do you prefer the guest who keeps telling you what a wonderful meal it is, but nibbles and refuses any more, or the guest who demolishes the first plateful . . . and then looks up appealingly for more? Verbal praise is empty flattery if it does not express a genuine appreciation of the object or person praised."[11]

We genuinely praise and love God when we take pleasure in God's creative love in those experiences that bring us joy and a sense of deep well-being. In these moments, we do not fret about our failures and sins or get overly anxious about what the future may hold. We are experiencing God's loving presence and the life God wants to give us, right now.

These moments of joy can be simple and ordinary. I began to experience the mystery of God's presence and activity with my first morning coffee as I took in its rich aroma, in the encouraging phone call from someone who had valued something I said, in the beauty of the flowers and shrubs of our small garden, in a warm hug from Debbie. All these kinds of down-to-earth experiences (and there are too many to mention) have touched my life with God's loving presence and brought much joy and aliveness.

One of the best ways to connect our sources of enjoyment with God's presence is to notice the gifts received through the day. Usually the best time to do this is just before going to sleep. Simply, we can ask the Lord to help us to see what we have really enjoyed through the day. Specific memories will usually come to mind. As we relive these special moments and savor these gifts, we imagine God's love streaming toward us in each one. We can then tell God how grateful we are for these moments. Returning to memories of gratitude has the power to strengthen our bodies, give us hope in times of disappointment, and deepen our sense of belonging to the God who loves us and cares for us.

What are your sources of joy? What makes you feel alive? What do you genuinely enjoy experiencing? These experiences are your unique gateways into seeking and finding God everywhere.

When you recognize this, a fresh sense of wonder and worship will flow through your life. You will want to offer yourself freely and wholeheartedly to the one who has loved you and this world into existence. This joyful surrender of your life to God will not arise out of any sense of obligation, duty, or fear. Rather, it will be the free expression of what is deepest in you as you experience God's loving and creative presence in all things. This is the life for which God has made you, the life which God alone can give you, the life which your heart seeks.

As we end, I invite you once again to offer yourself to God with the words of Ignatius's prayer:

Take, Lord, and receive all my liberty, my memory, my understanding, and all my will— all that I have and possess. You, Lord, have given all that to me. I now give it back to you, O Lord. All of it is yours. Dispose of it according to your will. Give me love of yourself along with grace, for that is enough for me.

AFTERWORD

AT RENOVARÉ—the spiritual-formation community where I work and the context in which I first got to know Trevor Hudson—we are always discovering that the most important things are "more caught than taught." We can talk about another kind of life in Jesus until we're blue in the face, but it's not until we see that life incarnated in the actions, postures, and presence of a fellow human being that we can begin to grasp what's possible.

When we *do* encounter that kind of life in someone else, it's downright contagious. If we don't immediately develop a full-blown case of what Trevor calls "the fullness of life that is the promise of the gospel," we will, at the very least, become infected with a serious longing for it. Saint Augustine observed this process of contagion and offered another, much lovelier metaphor to describe it: "One loving heart sets another on fire."[1]

In the wondrous book we have just read, Trevor has given us the gift of time with three such loving hearts—three

"God-soaked" lives crackling with the radiant fire of Jesus' presence. Two of these loving hearts are Trevor's good friends, Ignatius of Loyola and Dallas Willard. And the third, of course, is Trevor himself.

In case you have never met Trevor in person, let me assure you that he does indeed "live in the house of his own proclamation."[2] Trevor comes to North America twice a year to teach at the Renovaré Institute for Christian Spiritual Formation. Our students often report encountering Jesus so tangibly in Trevor's compassionate presence that they begin to hear the Lord speaking to them in a South African accent!

In response, Trevor is always quick with the reminder that each one of us is a singular word God speaks into the world. As surely as Ignatius, Dallas, and Trevor each embody another kind of life within their specific contexts, gifts, and circumstances, you and I are also invited to become a uniquely accented articulation of God's life and love.

What we all have in common, of course, is Jesus. What makes the lives of Ignatius, Dallas, and Trevor so compelling is their burning fascination with the Jesus we meet in the Gospels and their ongoing interaction with the Jesus who lives today.

My fellow God seeker, I'm willing to bet that the same Jesus who speaks to Ignatius, Dallas, and Trevor has been whispering to you. As you've read the pages of this book, perhaps a word has leaped off the page, a longing has come into focus, a distorted perception has been corrected, or the possibility of a new way of living has shimmered on the horizon in a fresh and compelling way. These inner stirrings have been nothing less than Jesus' own Spirit kindling your desire for him.

Rest assured, he is gradually making *your* heart the kind that sets others on fire.

Thanks be to God.

Carolyn Arends

For it is Christ's love that fuels our passion and holds us tightly, because we are convinced that he has given his life for all of us. This means all died with him, so that those who live should no longer live self-absorbed lives but lives that are poured out for him—the one who died for us and now lives again.

2 CORINTHIANS 5:14-15, TPT

ACKNOWLEDGMENTS

When it came to the writing and publication of this book, I owe heartfelt gratitude to three different communities.

First, to the NavPress community:

Dave Zimmerman, the present NavPress publisher, and Don Pape, who preceded him, for being willing to take the publishing risk with this project. Their confidence in my written words was a real gift when I wondered whether this book could be helpful for others.

Deborah Gonzalez, who went through the many revisions I needed to make in the manuscript, got the book ready for the copyediting process, and stayed in contact throughout this process.

Eric Stanford, who did the developmental editing, made numerous helpful suggestions, and encouraged me constantly "not to tell but to describe."

Elizabeth Schroll, whose careful copyediting, thoughtful suggestions, and wondering questions taught me so much about the craft of writing.

Ron Kaufmann, who invited my thoughts about the kind of

cover I wanted, came up with what you see, and left me hoping that the content would measure up to the cover's classical look.

Robin Bermel, who connected personally on Zoom, took time to listen to my hopes for the book, and offered creative marketing possibilities.

Olivia Eldredge, who collected the endorsements and helped me compile a list of influencers.

Second, to the Ignatian community, both in heaven and on earth:

Father Andrew Norton of the Community of the Resurrection, who took me through the full Spiritual Exercises in 1990 with care and competence.

Gerard Hughes, SJ, with whom I had the privilege of spending two weeks in the UK learning about the Spiritual Exercises in 1994.

William Barry, SJ, who accompanied me through the writing of this book, led me through an eight-day retreat, and wrote the foreword just before he died.

David Smolira, SJ, my first Jesuit spiritual director, from whom I learned so much about giving the Spiritual Exercises.

Russell Pollitt, SJ, and Dr. Annemarie Paulin-Campbell, from the Jesuit Community in South Africa, with whom I have enjoyed both friendship and colleagueship in sharing Ignatian treasures with others around the world.

Third, to my community of friends, colleagues, and family:

Bill Meaker, who invested hours in reading each chapter, correcting numerous grammatical mistakes, and helping me always find the simpler word.

The Willard family—Jane, Becky, and Bill—for taking time to read the book in its early stages and encouraging me to keep writing.

Dr. Gary Moon, for initiating the video series on which this book is based, writing a wonderful group study guide for the video series (which can also be profitably used with this book), and offering constant encouragement as I wrote.

Chris Hall, Lacy Borgo, Jean Nevills, Regina Moon, and Pam Stewart—colleagues at Fuller Seminary, where much of this book's content was shared in the DMin program in Spiritual Direction.

Carolyn Arends, for her generous afterword and for giving me the privilege of lecturing at the Renovaré Institute for Christian Spiritual Formation, where I have been able to explore Dallas Willard's key ideas with students.

Eff and Patti Martin, for their vision of bringing the voices of both Dallas Willard and Ignatius to a new generation through the Conversatio Devina website (https://conversatio.org) and the Martin Institute at Westmont University.

Richard Foster, for his thoughtful writings exploring the difference between *bios* life and *zoe* life, which have formed my imagination around the good news of Jesus.

And most especially to Debbie, my closest companion along the seeking Way, and to my children and their partners—Joni and James, Mark and Marike—who have always encouraged me in my writing efforts.

To God be the glory!

NOTES

CHAPTER 1: BECOMING A SEEKER

1. Brendan Busse, "Andrew Garfield Played a Jesuit in *Silence*, but He Didn't Expect to Fall in Love with Jesus," *America*, January 10, 2017, https://www.americamagazine.org/arts-culture/2017/01/10/andrew-garfield-played-jesuit-silence-he-didnt-expect-fall-love-jesus.
2. Dallas Willard, *The Divine Conspiracy: Rediscovering Our Hidden Life in God* (New York: HarperCollins, 1998), 370.

CHAPTER 2: SEEKING THE LIFE GOD GIVES

1. Paraphrased from "The Twelve Steps of Alcoholics Anonymous," accessed October 20, 2021, https://www.aa.org/assets/en_US/smf-121_en.pdf.
2. I have personalized his encouragement to say these words as he would say it in his talks. In *Divine Conspiracy* we have the sentence, "We are never-ceasing spiritual beings with an eternal destiny in the full world of God," Dallas Willard, *The Divine Conspiracy: Rediscovering Our Hidden Life in God* (New York: HarperCollins, 1998), 86.
3. Joseph Tylenda, *A Pilgrim's Journey: The Autobiography of Ignatius of Loyola* (San Francisco: Ignatius Press, 1985), 37–49.

CHAPTER 3: CHANGING DIRECTION

1. Pew Research Center, "In U.S., Decline of Christianity Continues at Rapid Pace," October 17, 2019, https://www.pewforum.org/2019/10/17/in-u-s-decline-of-christianity-continues-at-rapid-pace/.
2. "Why the Generations Approach Generosity Differently," Barna, June 19, 2019, https://www.barna.com/research/generations-generosity/.

3. Dallas Willard, *The Divine Conspiracy: Rediscovering Our Hidden Life in God* (New York: HarperCollins, 1998), 15.
4. Joseph Tylenda, *A Pilgrim's Journey: The Autobiography of Ignatius of Loyola* (San Francisco: Ignatius Press, 1985), 59–62.
5. Gary W. Moon, *Becoming Dallas Willard: The Formation of a Philosopher, Teacher, and Christ Follower* (Downers Grove, IL: IVP Books, 2018), 33–34.
6. Moon, *Becoming Dallas*, 43, 71.
7. Dallas Willard, "My Journey to and beyond Tenure in a Secular University," Faculty Forum Luncheon Remarks, C. S. Lewis Foundation Summer Conference, University of San Diego, June 21, 2003, https:// dwillard.org/articles/my-journey-to-and-beyond-tenure-in-a-secular -university.
8. Trevor Hudson, *Discovering Our Spiritual Identity: Practices for God's Beloved* (Downers Grove, IL: IVP, 2010), 29–30.

CHAPTER 4: DISCERNING OUR DEEPEST DESIRES

1. James Houston, *The Heart's Desire: A Guide to Personal Fulfillment* (Oxford, UK: Lion Publishing, 1992), 53.
2. David Fleming, *A Contemporary Reading of the Spiritual Exercises,* rev. ed. (St. Louis: Institute of Jesuit Sources, 1978), 7.
3. William Barry, *Letting God Come Close: An Approach to the Ignatian Spiritual Exercises* (Chicago: Loyola Press, 2001), 41.
4. Dallas Willard, *Renovation of the Heart* (Colorado Springs: NavPress, 2002), 57.
5. Quoted in Gary Moon, *Becoming Dallas Willard: The Formation of a Philosopher, Teacher, and Christ Follower* (Downers Grove, IL: IVP, 2018), 67.
6. Quoted in Moon, *Becoming Dallas*, 241.
7. This is a central idea in Dallas's thought. See *The Divine Conspiracy: Rediscovering Our Hidden Life in God* (New York: HarperCollins, 1998), 21–33.
8. Charles H. Spurgeon, "Ask and Have," in *Spurgeon's Sermons on Prayer* (Peabody, MA: Hendrickson, 2007), 109.
9. Gerard W. Hughes, *God in All Things* (London: Hodder & Stoughton, 2004), 74.
10. Margaret Magdalen, *Furnace of the Heart: Rekindling Our Longing for God* (London: Dartman, Longman & Todd, 1998), 4.

CHAPTER 5: EXPLORING LIFE'S GREATEST OPPORTUNITY

1. George A. Aschenbrenner, *Stretched for Greater Glory: What to Expect from the Spiritual Exercises* (Chicago: Loyola Press, 2004), 77.

2. William A. Barry, *Letting God Come Close: An Approach to the Ignatian Spiritual Exercises* (Chicago: Loyola Press, 2001), 77.

3. David L. Fleming, *The Spiritual Exercises of St. Ignatius: A Literal Translation and a Contemporary Reading* (St. Louis: Institute of Jesuit Sources, 1978), 27. My italics.

4. Dallas Willard, *Knowing Christ Today: Why We Can Trust Spiritual Knowledge* (New York: HarperOne, 2009), 141. Emphasis in original.

5. Fleming, *Spiritual Exercises of St. Ignatius*, 17.

6. I am in debt to William Barry for helping me understand the importance of mutual self-revelation in our relationship with God in Christ.

7. James Martin, *The Jesuit Guide to (Almost) Everything: A Spirituality for Real Life* (San Francisco: HarperOne, 2010), 126.

8. Dallas often used this paraphrase in his teaching. See also *Renewing the Christian Mind: Essays, Interviews and Talks*, ed. Gary Black Jr. (New York: HarperOne, 2016), 240: "Repent means to change the way you've been thinking and acting. Notice how you've been thinking, and then add to those thoughts the fact that it is now possible for you to begin living in God's kingdom right here, right where you are in this time of change and transition."

9. Dallas Willard, *The Great Omission: Reclaiming Jesus's Essential Teachings on Discipleship* (New York: HarperCollins, 2006), 10.

10. Dallas shared this story with me in a group setting.

CHAPTER 6: DYING TO LIVE

1. Dietrich Bonhoeffer, The Cost of Discipleship (London: SCM, 1959), 7.

2. N. T. Wright, *John for Everyone* (London: SPCK, 2002), 30.

3. "The boy's name was Jean-Marie Lustiger. He was admitted to the Catholic church the following Easter. And he became the Cardinal Archbishop of Paris. True story. He died on August 5th, 2007"; "You Did That for Me?" *Father Paul's Homily Blog*, March 28, 2010, http://frpaulhomilies.blogspot.com/2010/03/you-did-that-for-me.html.

4. Dallas Willard, *The Divine Conspiracy: Rediscovering Our Hidden Life in God* (San Francisco: HarperCollins, 1998), 334.

5. Dallas Willard explores this difference in *Life Without Lack: Living in the Fullness of Psalm 23* (Nashville: Nelson Books, 2018), 125–6.

6. Dallas Willard often would use this illustration. See *Renewing the Christian Mind: Essays, Interviews, and Talks* (New York: HarperOne, 2016), 270.

7. I am in debt here to the thinking of Mark Gibbard, SSJE.

8. Henri Nouwen, *Compassion: A Reflection on the Christian Life* (New York: Doubleday, 1982), 16.

9. David L. Fleming, *The Spiritual Exercises of St. Ignatius: A Literal Translation and a Contemporary Reading* (St. Louis: Institute of Jesuit Sources, 1978), 47.
10. William A. Barry, *Changed Heart, Changed World: The Transforming Freedom of Friendship with God* (Chicago: Loyola Press, 2011), 121.
11. Quoted in Gary W. Moon, *Becoming Dallas Willard: The Formation of a Philosopher, Teacher, and Christ Follower* (Downers Grove, IL: IVP, 2018), 150–151.

CHAPTER 7: EXPERIENCING RESURRECTION JOY

1. Gary W. Moon, *Becoming Dallas Willard: The Formation of a Philosopher, Teacher, and Christ Follower* (Downers Grove, IL: IVP, 2018), 131.
2. While I develop it in different ways, the idea of finding common features in the Resurrection stories of the Gospels comes from Gerard W. Hughes, *God of Surprises* (London: Darton, Longman & Todd, 1985).
3. Dallas Willard in Trevor Hudson, *Hope Beyond Your Tears: Experiencing Christ's Healing Love* (Nashville: Upper Room Books, 2012), 7.
4. I also wrote about this in *Hope Beyond Your Tears: Experiencing Christ's Healing Love* (Nashville: Upper Room, 2012), 95.
5. Personal correspondence with the Reverend Rowan Rogers, minister in the Methodist Church of Southern Africa.
6. Hughes, *God of Surprises*, 94.
7. See David L. Fleming, *The Spiritual Exercises of St. Ignatius: A Literal Translation and a Contemporary Reading* (St. Louis: Institute of Jesuit Sources, 1978), 76–77.
8. See Fleming, *The Spiritual Exercises of St. Ignatius*, 76.
9. Fleming, *The Spiritual Exercises of St. Ignatius*, 77.

CHAPTER 8: FINDING GOD IN ALL THINGS

1. David L. Fleming, *The Spiritual Exercises of St. Ignatius: A Literal Translation and a Contemporary Reading* (St. Louis: Institute of Jesuit Sources, 1978), 56.
2. Fleming, *The Spiritual Exercises of St. Ignatius*, 56.
3. William A. Barry, *Letting God Come Close: An Approach to the Ignatian Spiritual Exercises* (Chicago: Loyola Press, 2001), 183.
4. My paraphrase of Fleming, *The Spiritual Exercises of St. Ignatius*, 56.
5. Fleming, *The Spiritual Exercises of St. Ignatius*, 57.
6. My paraphrase of Fleming, *The Spiritual Exercises of St. Ignatius*, 56.
7. Michael Ivens, *Understanding the Spiritual Exercises: Text and Commentary: A Handbook for Retreat Directors* (Leominster, UK: Gracewing, 1998), 177.
8. I am in debt to Father Gerard W. Hughes, SJ, for the term *split spirituality*, which he uses in his many writings.

9. "Letter to Father Antonio Brandao," in *Ignatius of Loyola: Letters and Instructions*, ed. John W Padberg (St. Louis: Institute of Jesuit Sources, 1996), 339–45. Thanks to Father Matthew Charlesworth, SJ, for tracking down this quotation for me.
10. Personal correspondence with Dallas Willard.
11. Gerard Hughes, *God of Surprises* (London: Darton, Longman & Todd, 1985), 56.

AFTERWORD

1. Augustine, *De Cat. Rud.*, 13.19.209, as cited in Richard J. Foster, *Streams of Living Water: Essential Practices from the Six Great Traditions of Christian Faith* (San Francisco: HarperSanFrancisco, 2001), 195.
2. Trevor often suggests that as Christ followers, we are called to "live in the house of our own proclamation."

NavPress is the book-publishing arm of The Navigators.

Since 1933, The Navigators has helped people around the world bring hope and purpose to others in college campuses, local churches, workplaces, neighborhoods, and hard-to-reach places all over the world, face-to-face and person-by-person in an approach we call Life-to-Life® discipleship. We have committed together to know Christ, make Him known, and help others do the same.®

Would you like to join this adventure of discipleship and disciplemaking?

- Take a Digital Discipleship Journey at **navigators.org/disciplemaking**.
- Get more discipleship and disciplemaking content at **thedisciplemaker.org**.
- Find your next book, Bible, or discipleship resource at **navpress.com**.

 @NavPressPublishing

 @NavPress

 @navpressbooks

CP1790